2023,

THE PEOPLE'S EMERGENCY ACT

TOM MARAZZO

ISBN-13: 978-1-7380671-1-4

Dedication

This book is dedicated to the brave hearts and steady hands that became the backbone of the Freedom Convoy.

To my two children, who have always been my guiding stars, the embodiment of a better future, and the inspiration behind every action I take.

To the fearless Canadians who initiated the Convoy, reminding us that we always possess the means to fight for what we believe in.

To the steadfast truckers, who braved the bitter cold of Ottawa, living in their vehicles for days on end, becoming the pulse of this monumental movement.

To the loved ones who kept the home fires lit, their unwavering support echoing through every mile and every moment.

To the devoted parents, who bound by their sacred oaths to their children, strove to sculpt a better world for future generations.

To the Doctors and Lawyers who held fast to their professional vows, risking everything to ensure that truth and justice were not mere concepts, but living realities.

And finally, to the brave men and women who became Canada's Political Prisoners - your courage under fire has etched a lasting mark on the annals of our nation's history.

This is a humble tribute to each one of you. Your stories, your sacrifices, and your unwavering commitment have not only inspired this book, but continue to inspire countless Canadians.

Table of Contents

Foreword

"I" and "think" are two words as small and seemingly innocuous as any can be.

Put them together and they have the power to question, to resist, to make a declaration, to define oneself, to mobilize a people into resistance and sometimes even victory.

To think is not just to ruminate or wallow in introspection. It is not mere entertainment. And it is not an inherently selfish act. It defines who and what we are, as individuals and as a people. A human without the capacity to think, without things to think about or reasons to think for oneself is an empty shell of what she was or might have been.

René Descartes, who famously quipped, "I think, therefore I am," recognized the power of putting these two little words together. "I think" allowed him to question all that could possibly be untrue, to tear down the whole system of knowledge that buttressed the institutions of his time, and to build his knowledge up again from sure foundations. These two little words became the slogan, if you will, of the period we now call the Enlightenment (the intellectual movement that defined the 17th and 18th centuries).

Unfortunately, the lessons of the Enlightenment didn't stick.

Despite the efforts of many, we now find ourselves recoiling to an intellectual dark age defined by one official narrative, bullies who insidiously defend it, and the shaming, blaming and even termination of those who dare to question it.

I think so.

I think not.

I want to think a little more about that.

I want to think for myself.

Who knew how powerful, how threatening, even how traitorous these words could be.

Yet here we find ourselves in a hellish reality that the Freedom Convoy made poignant to us. Canada no longer feels like home. It is no longer a safe haven. Neighbours feel like strangers. Families are torn apart. Parents are struggling to feed their families, to educate their children, to navigate a crumbling health care system. Our flag waves weakly and "Best country in the world" are now empty words.

On a frigid day in February, 2022, I was driving on Highway 7 on my way to Ottawa, two days after the Freedom Convoy arrived in the city's core. We were in deep winter, snow bending evergreen boughs and piles of icy slurry pushed to the sides of the road. The glare from the sun on the road made it hard to see. My nerves grew as I got closer and closer to Ottawa.

Trucks passed me in the other direction, with Canada flags strapped to their grill or tied to hockey sticks waving out the back. There were the customary honks and waves as we passed, but I had no idea what would await me when I got to the downtown core.

Getting to the city outskirts was one thing; but I then had to navigate through the blockaded streets to my downtown hotel, which proved to be impossible. I found an empty parking lot blocks away and meandered through idling trucks, street parties and people walking with flags tied around their shoulders, hugging, and cheering as they passed.

As I walked the frigid streets, along Wellington in front of Parliament Hill, across the Rideau Canal, and in front of the National War Memorial, spirits were high and the mood was light, despite subzero temperatures. Piles of donated food, available for any trucker who needed it, were stacked in front of trucks parked near intersections.

I met a beautiful pair of couples — one French, one English, neither of which could speak the others' language well, but who had become friends — sharing meals, conversation, and a hotel room for the night, to shower and rest. There was music and happiness, a feeling of community and a sense of relief that something was finally being done. Music played, people danced, children sang and waved little paper flags.

So this is a Convoy, I thought.

I walked over to the Supreme Court one morning — a cold, imposing structure set well back from the road — feeling a sense of irony that there was such a disconnect between our government and the people in the streets, as there often is when a society starts to fall apart.

I was invited to visit the trucker headquarters where I saw Danny Bulford talking amicably with police liaisons at the entrance. Once inside, I saw a calm, positive scene, clearly well-organized. No sign of distress or uncertainty. Ample coffee, fingers typing furiously, maps, schedules, and a well-stocked buffet.

Even now, 17 months later, I remember the biting cold. I took the warmest clothes I had but my hands and feet would ache after just a few minutes. I didn't know how the Truckers were managing. But they weren't just managing. They were thriving. They were singing and playing games and rallying, and clearing snow and ice off the sidewalks so people could pass. Garbage bags hung on the iron railings on Wellington and I was offered coffee or chili or gloves whenever I walked about.

What I saw in Ottawa was, in short, a very different world from what appeared on the news. I didn't get any of this information second-hand. I didn't read it in a blog. I didn't hear it from an anchor. This is what I saw. This is what I felt.

I first met Tom Marazzo on the deck of a bucolic farm on the Niagara escarpment, so remote that I got lost on my way there because my phone lost a signal before I finished navigating. I had to 'old-school' stop and ask the straw-hatted gentleman scything something in a ditch, which worked as well as any GPS.

I was there to be interviewed for a documentary about the Convoy. The film crew were gathered, including Jeremy Regot and Andrew Peloso, interviewees, the farm owners — themselves freedom volunteers — and friends. A group of about fifteen in total.

I didn't really know who Tom was. I vaguely remembered seeing him during some of the Convoy press conferences, but I didn't know what his role was, or how he was connected to Danny Bulford or Tamara Lich. We were quietly introduced, reaching to shake hands across a large patio table.

Tom doesn't have the face, or the wardrobe, of a freedom fighter, or a fighter of any kind. He is conspicuously inconspicuous. Unassuming in a reliable Oxford shirt and khakis, always with recently barbered hair. Gentle, thoughtful, well spoken. Empathetic. Clear and focused in his conversation. A good listener. You would never know from looking at him that he was an army Captain or that he has a black belt in Krav Maga.

In fact, very few of those who led the Convoy in Ottawa, and who continue to fight for our freedom in quieter ways now, are not obviously bigger or tougher than anyone else. Their courage if anything, is quiet, but reliable. If you put Tom Marazzo, Danny Bulford, and Tamara Lich in a room with 100 others, you would never pick *them* out as leaders of a movement that captured the world's attention. They were not obvious Goliaths but quiet Davids to our government's brutishness.

This fact teaches an important lesson. Both heroes and villains can come from the common and unassuming. As Hannah Arendt remarked about the demeanor of Holocaust organizer, Adolf Eichmann, he did not appear to be a brilliant, diabolical figure responsible for the organization and termination of millions; instead, he was a diminutive man just following orders, commonly banal, while capable of uncommon evil.

Heroism too, can be found in the person next door, the mother desperate to protect her children, the Trucker who can't bear what is happening to his country, the father of a vaccine injured child who is keenly aware of the harms that can be done by even our most reputable institutions.

One thing that struck me about the Convoy in general was the diversity of the group.

There were truckers, yes, but also scientists and academics, lawyers, journalists, members of the military, elderly couples, families with young children. There were conservatives, liberals,

Green Party members. Whites, Hispanics, Indians.

As I wandered, I wondered what brought this seemingly disparate group of people to our nation's capital for thirty-three days in the depth of winter. What made us unite over this particular issue? What brought people to a Saskatchewan overpass as one arm of the Convoy passed underneath? What created a watershed of donations as the Convoy traveled across the country? What made people give up their jobs and the security of their homes to live in frigid conditions without showers or food, and in the end, no fuel, for over a month? What mobilized a country?

Was the Convoy about vaccine mandates? On the surface, yes. Young and old, trucker or not, vaccinated or not, those who headed to Ottawa felt very deeply that the government had overstepped by imposing COVID-19 vaccine mandates and that the citizens who went along with this overstep were wrong to do so.

But, even more general than that, they all seemed to feel that our way of life was being threatened and that something needed to be done.

If I had to pinpoint the commonality between all the Convoy participants, I'd say it's that their demeanors bely a more complex and deep backstory. Many have had to fight for truth, know the costs, and would gladly pay them again. Addiction, family strife, war, extreme illness, escaping communism … the list goes on. Tom has been through medical hell with his children. Others fled to Canada as a safe haven from a repressive regime. Some are just keenly aware of historical atrocities and see their early signs now.

Whatever their reason, these people's instincts for oppression and harm are so carefully honed that, when things started to go wrong in 2020, they recognized it immediately. And they knew that the costs of doing nothing would incur a debt we wouldn't be able to pay.

So, why write a book about the Convoy now? Do words really matter at a time when dissenting opinions are simply ignored and sometimes erased altogether? Why write in a culture of silence and deep cancelation?

This is a question that answers itself. You speak, you write, precisely when your culture is the most silent. That's when your words are needed most. You write because doing so is the antidote to cancelation, because speaking up is the antidote to fear. You write because you refuse to be terrorized, gaslit, and erased.

Perhaps the greatest gift of the Convoy is that resisting the narrative served to reveal the insistence of it. If we lived in a truly free society, one in which dissenting ideas could tread safely into the public sphere, hang out for a while, and then give way to a new problem, dissenters wouldn't be targets. But the COVID narrative has been irrationally buoyant. It stood the test of time in spite of every reason to sink. And its buoyancy quickly and efficiently throws dissenters overboard.

The more people write and speak against the narrative, the

more its irrationality will reveal itself. Witnessing the harms of the Covid response should awaken us to the unintended consequences of converting science into Scientism, and its practitioners into unthinking defenders of it. It's been a litmus test not just of individual will-power and independent thought but of the power of an idea, asserted consistently and insidiously enough that evidence and discussion are seen as anything from frivolous distraction to a dangerous threat to public safety. Writing is part of resisting. It's part of telling our stories, of giving moral attention to the ignored, the shamed, the unseen, and unheard.

As Trish Wood elegantly said, "We change history by telling stories." The Freedom Convoy Commission, the National Citizen's Inquiry. Tamara Lich's *Hold the Line*, every freedom interview, podcast, and Substack article. Every conversation with friends.

This is Tom Marazzo's story of twenty-two days in Ottawa that captured the world's attention. Twenty-two days that Canadian people went to the foot of government and refused to be ignored. Twenty-two days that will forever be part of our history.

Tom's book is a testimony to a powerful experience that many of us shared.

What is the point of testimony?

To get at truth? Possibly. There is an important epistemic value to testimony. It can introduce new information into the public sphere. It can invite others to imaginatively engage with our experience. Testimony is a story not just about events but about the motivation behind those events, what it felt like to live them, and how it changed people. But testimony aims at more than just truth.

Testimony also helps to create some order out of the chaos of our experiences even to the point of experiencing catharsis on the page. Dani Shapiro says that writing has a way of shaping the chaos, "looking at all the pieces side-by-side so they make more sense." Tom wrote to me in July 2023, "What an ordeal. Writing this book has taken a lot out of me. It was very difficult. I feel like I lived the Convoy three times: the actual, the POEC, and the book." Telling our stories can be an important way to bring order — emotional, psychological order — to our experiences.

And finally telling our stories brings moral attention to them. As Susan Sontag wrote, "To be a moral human being is to pay, be obliged to pay, certain kinds of attention." At a time when so many of us are ignored and silenced, moral attention is needed now more than ever.

To speak and write any dissenting opinion today is an act of courage. Tom's actions in Ottawa were an act of courage. His walk with James Topp was an act of courage. Writing this book is an act of courage.

Courage takes many forms. Sometimes it comes from the one "in front" who leads the battle cry. Sometimes it comes in the form of military advances and nuclear weapons.

Sometimes it is the quiet persistence of mothers who defend their children, or children who create imaginary worlds to cope with the world's brutishness. And sometimes it comes from an unassuming college professor who heeds the words of John F Kennedy who said, "We use power or power uses us."

Tom does not know everything. I do not know everything. But we each know some small thing, which is that the attention we give one another and each other's stories, especially in times of crisis, says almost all we need to know about our humanity.

If you are reading this and you think that you can just fly under the radar and find safety in silence and compliance, that staying quiet will make it all go away, heed the words of Camus who said, "Silence has dangerous implications."

Silence will not get us off this particular moral hook. We must tell our stories when we have them. And the more others try to silence us, the more important it is that we tell them.

We are still writing the chapters of this awful event in history, and we don't know yet how the story will turn out. But I do know that how history will remember us will have a lot to do with how we write our story now, with what we leave on the page, with what we have the courage to say…and to do.

We think. Therefore, we are.

Thinking — reflecting, questioning, telling our stories. This is what defines us.

Let the story telling begin.

Julie Ponesse, Ph.D.

Acknowledgements

The creation of this book has been a dance of dedication, passion, and unity. It has involved a multitude of talented and committed individuals, each with a role that has been instrumental in bringing this work to life.

Mary Giuffre, my story editor, your drive and determination surpass my own. You believed in this book even before it was a tangible reality, and I am deeply grateful for your relentless persistence and faith.

Paul Clark, you have brilliantly captured the essence of this work through the book cover.

Maria Abramov, your photographic skills have elevated my image beyond the ordinary, a feat that only a truly gifted artist can achieve.

A special thanks to Lisa Robbins, our technical editor. Your precision and attention to detail have enriched and clarified this narrative, making it accessible and engaging.

Keith Wilson and Eva Chipiuk, your companionship during the Convoy in Ottawa and the tumultuous times at the POEC has been a source of strength and comfort. I could not have asked for better comrades.

Brendan Miller and Bath-Shéba van den Berg, your unbridled spirit, and what I call a delicious shade of insanity, led us through the challenges at the POEC. You're both insane lawyers, and it's the kind of insanity I admire!

Julie Ponesse, Ph.D., your forward sets a powerful tone for the rest of the book, and I am grateful for your thoughtful contribution.

In memory of Steve Rigney, a friend whose generosity and brilliance shone in every endeavor. From aiding with a book website to supporting a Provincial Campaign, Steve's contributions were endless. Though taken from the world too soon, his spirit lives on in the hearts of those he touched. Rest in peace, dear friend. You are missed.

To all the individuals who were part of the Freedom Convoy - Andrew Peloso, Chantelle, Chris V, Chris, Christine Anderson,

Clyde, Dale, Dan S, Dana, Danny and Piper, Decks, Derek Sloan, Derek Smith, Eddie, Harold, Jack, James Peloso, James Topp, James, Jeff B, Jeremy R, John Fuel, Joseph Bourgault, Karl, Kirsten Kelly, Laura and Patrick, Leanne, Lola, Martin, Mike and Vickie, Mike C, Mike Stack, Miranda, Paul, Ray, Rick S, Roger, Roy and Nicole, Roy, Ryan Olsen, Sandy, Sean, Shawn Buckley, Tamara, Tasha, Teehan, Terry, Thomas, Tim, Vince, Wendy, you've left an indelible mark on this book and my life.

Joanna Wilczek, you've been my rock through this journey, especially the last and most difficult leg. Without your unwavering support and your infectious smile, the completion of this book would have remained a distant dream.

Lastly, to 'The Canadian Trucker', and all those not listed but held dear in my memory, your support and contributions have been invaluable.

I express my deepest gratitude to all of you. This book, in its entirety, is a testament to your support, talent, and dedication.

Thank you. Tom.

Preface

If I try really hard to find my inner most compassion, I can understand why so many people around the world turned on their loved ones, friends, and colleagues – because of the anchorman and his fear. When the pandemic started, you could literally watch the media manipulations. They were not reporting news, they were reporting fear. It was a very obvious campaign of terrorism by our own media, pumped into our TVs and smart phones.

In December of 2019, I remember listening to the CBC while driving to the College, where I was about to teach a class. One of the now infamous Provincial Chief Medical Officers was comparing Covid-19 to influenza and saying there was nothing to worry about.

As we moved into March 2020, I was given a heads up by a friend that Canada was going to do a lockdown, two weeks before it actually happened. Yes it's true, I'm the one who bought all of the toilet paper before you even had a chance!

As the days went by, the news would report twenty cases per day of Covid-19 and then after about a week it was 200 cases per day. Eventually it was 2,000 cases of Covid-19 per day. The only reason I kept looking was because I couldn't understand the media's fascination with "cases", compared to hospital admissions, ICU admissions and fatalities.

The media was only reporting fear, and grossly out of context with almost no analysis. The "number" was all that seemed to be required to terrify the public as much as possible, except some of us could see right through it.

It was my opinion that the fear was meant to get people to comply with new restrictions and to also get the public to do the dirty work of snitching and shaming those who saw through the obvious Covid-19 charade. None of the new rules or fines made any logical sense, but a counter to obvious logic was to use shame and even more fear. We were told that if we didn't follow the rules, our innocent children would be killing their grandparents. The list of absurdities regarding the guilt tactics used, could fill another book.

I had talked to a long-time friend who I did my officer

training with, in the Canadian Army, and I said, "I don't know what is really going on, but I know what we're being told is a lie." That was the last time we spoke, and we had been friends for over twenty years.

My son has been in and out of hospitals all his young life, so I am very aware of the concept of Informed Consent. As his father, I've had to sit with doctors and go over all the risks associated with a procedure or operation he was about to have. I needed to be "informed" of the risks, to then grant my "consent" on his behalf. It is a two-part formula. The doctor must inform a patient of the risks and recommended treatment. The patient or guardian must sign a document stating that they fully understand the risks being presented to you. Then, and only then, are you allowed to give consent.

With the Covid-19 injections, the "informed" part of this equation was impossible to give because there is no long-term safety data in existence.

My son has autism. His mother and I have already forgotten more about autism, than most people will ever have to learn. I left Facebook a few years before the pandemic because I was tired of getting into arguments with people over vaccines. I heard the typical phrases like, "correlation doesn't mean causation" with the almighty references to the Polio vaccine saving all the children of the world. I had a doctor once tell me that that one study about vaccines and autism was "debunked". The moment he used that phrase, I knew he hadn't read the Dr. Andrew Wakefield study. He obviously didn't know there were twelve other doctors on that study, including Professor John Walker-

Smith who was the former department head at the Royal Free Hospital in north London. Professor John Walker-Smith was regarded as the Godfather of gastrointestinal medicine in the U.K.

Celebrity Jenny McCarthy who also has a son with autism, wrote a book about her experiences with vaccines. Her son Evan almost died when the MMR vaccine was administered in a pediatrician's office. As hard as she tried, the media, special interests, and the public at large, shouted her down. She was trying to tell her story, and she was vilified by almost everyone, except for other families who had similar stories of autism and their children. Jenny also co-authored a book with a pediatrician who had a vaccine injured son with autism. I know many parents of once perfectly healthy children who were given the MMR vaccine. That was the day their lives changed forever, and they became members of the autistic community.

Despite overwhelming eyewitness evidence, coupled with the Vaccine Adverse Event Reporting System (VAERS), the general public still thinks that vaccines are risk free. In fact, if you choose not to vaccinate your children, the general consensus is, that you should be forced to do so, or have them taken away from you. People are absolutely willing to let you roll the dice with the health and lives of your kids, in order to protect people who are already vaccinated and apparently already protected against the viruses they've been vaccinated for!

What most people don't understand is that the greatest impact to eradicating most known viruses is not vaccines. Its actually the clean drinking water that is plumbed into the homes of every first world nation on Earth. Do you ever wonder why it's recommended that you get a booster before traveling to a third world country? It's because they don't have sewage treatment plants, clean drinking water, and good personal hygiene! Big pharmaceutical companies love to take credit for saving us from viruses. It makes you wonder how humanity even survived at all, without vaccinations!

I knew the Covid-19 pandemic was nothing more than a way for the government to get people to voluntarily inject themselves with a new, experimental drug. Fear is a big motivator, but the master plan by the government was to capitalize and weaponize the public's belief system about vaccines. If a doctor advocated for the vaccine, they'd be held up as heroic patriots. If they questioned what the government was doing, their credentials were not attacked, but their sanity was. If you agreed, you were a hero. If you actually exercised medical ethics and tried to apply the rigorous scientific methods that had been practiced for generations, you would be deemed a "quack" by your licensing board and cowardly, corrupt peers. Years of schooling and impeccable credentials only mattered if you agreed with the government. Despite reports of ongoing "vax related" illnesses, injuries, and deaths, as of the writing of this book, the Liberal government position has not changed.

For a short time, I went out in public wearing a mask. I didn't believe it was effective, but I also didn't want to draw any attention to myself in those early days. I took a wait and see approach while I gathered data on what was really happening. It was baffling to me to learn that a virus can tell if you are walking to your restaurant table with a mask, then completely leave you alone when you arrive at your chair and remove your mask. But it knew you were going to the washroom, so mask on. At the height of the lockdowns, you could only get the absolute bare essentials, but government owned booze was okay to purchase at the LCBO – Liquor Control Board of Ontario. You could go to a packed Walmart, but not a small retailer, who could actually control the number of customers entering their business. When people started to complain about this, Walmart stopped selling certain non-essential items and then decided to section off certain products in the store. The covid-19 virus was so smart, it could tell the difference between baby clothes and underwear. The irony was that the areas sectioned off, were already in the store and on the shelves, but because Covid-19 was so smart, and we're not, you just can't buy certain products, or you would become one of the 2,000 daily cases.

I remember when the government started targeting Christian churches, and arresting pastors. I saw people saying that if the government was going to close down your church, go to Walmart and hold your service there!

Yet, we were all told to follow the "science". Shameful.

Seeing what I was seeing, I mistakenly thought the lawyers in this country were going to put a stop to all this madness. A few did. Most didn't. In fact, it was lawyers who wrote the policies, mandates, and by-laws to lock us all down and created fines in the thousands of dollars. People were literally kidnapped by authorities and taken to quarantine facilities against their will.

I watched a Rebel News story about a woman in Alberta who was taken into custody after getting off a plane, by so called authorities, and brought to an undisclosed location in an unmarked SUV. They even refused to tell her husband where they were taking her. Had that been me being taken into custody, I would have refused to go with them and fought like my life depended on it. I would never have submitted to a quarantine facility under any circumstances. I have a black belt in Krav Maga, so I like my chances.

Not long after the pandemic started, I saw a video from a man named Lieutenant-Colonel David Redmen, retired. He was the former head of Emergency Management Alberta or EMA. His video was a scathing inditement of the way all the provinces had been handling the pandemic. After sending letters, he was completely ignored by all the provincial Premiers and the federal government. To top it off, even EMA completely ignored him. I knew he was right, and I also knew of the existence of EMO, Emergency Management Ontario.

The reason I knew about EMO, was because they have a Liaison Officer at the Army Headquarters in Toronto, Ontario, and I sat beside him during the morning briefs with the Division Commander when I was posted there in 2008-2010. Every fall, the HQ does a weeklong domestic operations exercise, and EMO is a significant part of that process. This was how I came to learn about one of the Canadian military's contingency plans called Operation Lazer. Op Lazer is the Army's contingency plan for pandemics, and I had to review it annually.

When Redmen was talking in the video, he clearly outlined what the roles of the government elected officials were and what they should have been doing. They didn't do any of it. In fact, as

Redmen recalled, they did everything they were not supposed to do, and what was counter to the World Health Organization's best practices. Even the WHO knew that masks were unnecessary, and lockdowns had a catastrophic effect on the economy and mental health, to say nothing of the fact that the children, who were least at risk, were over protected, and the elderly, who were at great risk, were not properly protected. Each provincial Premier is the legal authority and the decision maker, not their bureaucratic Chief Medical Officers. Instead, each Premier abdicated their duties and responsibilities to these unelected bureaucrats, who had no idea what they were doing.

To understand how it was supposed to work, I'll explain it like a wheel. In the center of the wheel is a hub that holds the spokes. That hub is the provincial Emergency Management Office, and every Province and Territory has one. The EMO would have co-ordinated the considerations from each of the spokes, like police, medical, financial, education, religious leaders, etc. The situation would have been monitored and managed by EMO, using a method called the Operational Planning Process and each Premier would have been provided regular situational awareness, through information briefings every twelve to twenty-four hours. When a decision was required, the EMO would have done a full analysis and given the Premier clear options with recommendations to inform their best possible decision. That's how it was always intended to work, but that's not what any Premier did.

Each Premier took their Chief Medical Officer out of the spoke position and put them at the center of the wheel as the hub. Their mission was to protect what they knew - the medical system. They had one goal. Protect the hospitals at all costs, no matter the outcome – because that's all they understood. The Federal Government did the exact same stupid thing.

To me, this was never about science or medicine, it was always about the laws in Canada, which exist to protect the public from medical malpractice and government malfeasance. Informed Consent is so paramount in medicine that it comes with criminal charges if violated. Yet, every level of Government coerced people to undergo a medical procedure they didn't want. The Canadian Privacy Act was also violated with impunity. Medical privacy protections also exist, yet any employee of a business was told they could refuse unvaccinated people entry, for not revealing medical information.

Section 6, Mobility Rights, of the Canadian Charter of Rights and Freedoms was absolutely violated by the provinces as well as the feds. When the Charter was written, a pandemic was considered as a possible reason to deny a Canadian's rights to travel to and from Canada, or to other Provinces. That was rejected outright, as not being a justifiable reason to deny Canadian's their right to move around their own country. But during the pandemic, our governments did it anyway.

There are so many laws in place to protect us from what the governments did to us all, yet very few from the legal community were immune to the fear coming from the media. What many people don't realize is that the Canadian Charter of Rights and Freedoms has one purpose – to protect the citizens from the governments. You can only bring a Charter challenge against an agent of a government. You can't go after a private company for a Charter violation.

Canada is also a country that has adopted the 10 Principles of the Nuremberg Code, and these are the basis for Health Canada regulations when it comes to medical experimentation. The first Principle is: "The voluntary consent of the human subject is absolutely essential."

Being told you would not be permitted to participate in society if you did not accept the Covid-19 experimental injection was of form of pure coercion and extortion.

We have laws, specifically meant to protect us from government overreach, even during a pandemic. We have provincial organizations, trained, prepared, and equipped to deal with a pandemic. Yet, every institution in our society succumbed to fear and all laws and critical thinking evaporated instantly – because of the fear we were bombarded with every single hour of every day.

I kept my head down and secretly made alliances and arrangements with unvaccinated people who could see we were being lied to but were still unable to break through the wall of fear that had gripped so many of their friends and family. Parents turned on their children and children turned on their parents and siblings. The RCMP set up a snitch line, so we could tell on our neighbors who didn't follow the rules. I learned that many of the people I thought would have fought back against the Nazi's, would actually have been staunch collaborators. I learned this when the faculty at Georgian College rebelled against me.

The pressure on six million unvaccinated Canadians was too

great and something had to give. In the early days, Truckers in Canada were held up by the government, as unsung heroes. It was the same with our nurses. Then one day, Truckers were told they could do a cross boarder trip to the USA, but then had to quarantine for fourteen days upon their return home, even if they didn't exit their trucks! They couldn't make a living under those conditions. Let's just say, the actions of the federal government, toward the Canadian Truckers, was highly motivating and was the perfect opportunity for me to come out of being a grey man and to finally get involved. I didn't know what the answer was before the Convoy, but I immediately recognized it for what it was, the moment I learned about it.

This is my story of how I finally found an opportunity to fight for the future of my children. For that, I will always owe the courageous Canadian Truckers a debt of gratitude.

Introduction

It's been over a year since the end of the Freedom Convoy in Ottawa and my life has forever been drastically changed. Despite the unprecedented challenge that the Covid-19 pandemic has imposed on our lives, I never anticipated that I would have found myself at the middle of so much turmoil in our nation's history.

Originally, I hoped to publish this book, on the one-year anniversary of the declaration of The Emergencies Act that Prime Minister Justin Trudeau invoked against the Freedom Convoy, on February 14, 2022. The irony of the Convoy's title – The Freedom Convoy – concluded with a violent outcome we didn't expect to see in a country like Canada. With full suspension of the Charter of Rights and Freedoms, for the crime of protesting our government's overreach, and the vilification of ordinary Canadians. For ten days, the Canadian Charter of Rights and Freedoms had no meaning in this country. The bank accounts of 280 Canadians, were frozen without warrants for our arrest, criminal charges, or any convictions, mine included. I could not purchase my son's heart medication for ten days. If not for his mother having cash to refill his prescription, he might not have gotten his medication.

As part of the legislation, when The Emergencies Act is invoked, a Commission must be held and a report is due to the Government, as well as Parliament, within 360 days of revocation of the Act. This is part of the legislation itself and must take place under law. Of course, Trudeau has tried to spin it as if he called for it as a wise and benevolent leader. He didn't have a choice!

The Commission was named the Public Order Emergency Commission, or POEC for short. It took place from October 13 to November 25, 2022 and the Commissioner was an Ontario Court of Appeal Judge named Paul Rouleau.

My original intention was to tell this story, before the time of the POEC, but I realized that it would not provide the complete picture. I sat in the POEC audience in person, for the entire seven weeks, and I also testified as a witness.

Originally, I wanted to tell this story with a few goals in mind. One, I only wanted to write what I personally witnessed. I wanted to treat it as if I had a Go-Pro on my head and that if the camera didn't record it, I wouldn't write about it. After listening to the POEC testimony, I realized the story would be incomplete with my Go-Pro approach.

Two, I had no intention of criticizing anyone, on our team. We were all there for the right reasons, which I originally believed. However, after listening to the testimony of some of the witnesses, I will have to rely on what I heard from them and let the reader decide if I'm being fair or not to that person. There is one caveat; I will not be kind to any member of the federal Liberal Cabinet for what they have done to this country and to the Freedom Convoy.

Like millions of Canadians, I've lost a lot in terms of personal relationships I once had, but I've also gained a new family of patriots who see what is happening to humanity and they're not going down without a fight.

I didn't start the Convoy. It wasn't even my idea. Like many of you reading this book, I was glued to social media to keep up to date on what was happening and to see how I could support it. You could say I was simply an inspired Canadian like everyone else. I even donated to the GoFundMe campaign to support the Convoy in a small way.

I've often been asked about how I got involved with the Freedom Convoy, and to answer that question I need to go back to September of 2021, when I was fired from my teaching job at Georgian College in Barrie, Ontario. The bizarre sequence of events that resulted because of that termination, to me, is akin to being struck by lightening or winning the lottery!

I started teaching software, at Georgian College, in September of 2019, immediately after graduating from Seneca College with a Degree in software development.

After medically retiring from the military in 2015, I was on my second career. Everything was going really well, and I worked very hard to be the best teacher I could be. Software is incredibly abstract, so I focused on reducing complicated concepts down to their simplest forms.

At the beginning of the January 2020 semester, I submitted a proposal to the Dean, to start a multi-disciplinary club to modify electric three-wheeled vehicles, built by past students. This new club would focus on making them self-driving. I enrolled in the Udacity, self-driving car online course, and the college agreed to let me start the club.

During my degree program at Seneca, I discovered I have a real love for computer vision, so for me this was a very exciting project. Also, Georgian College was starting a new one-year diploma program in artificial intelligence. Additionally, Georgian has a strong relationship to Honda Canada because of their factory in Alliston, Ontario. It was a win-win for everyone, and it was something that was going to help me eventually get a full-time teaching job. The day I found out about the first lock-down, I had just completed my very first student meeting for the new club. That was the first, and only meeting we had because the lockdowns put an end to all on-campus learning for over a year, especially for the software people.

As we went into the lock-down, we immediately converted to on-line classes, and I could see the constant stress it was putting the students under and trying to continue with the self-driving vehicle project was just too much.

In August of 2021, both Western University and Seneca College, implemented their own vaccine mandates. In what later became a very high-profile dismissal from Western University, an Ethics Professor named Dr. Julie Ponesse went viral with a video that outlined why she believed the vaccine mandates were unethical. Like many others, I too shared the video because it was brilliant and very emotional. Most people who watched it, including me, choked back a few tears at the end of that video along with Dr. Ponesse. It was particularly concerning to me personally because soon afterward, I received a text from the co-ordinator of the program I was teaching in. He forewarned that when Seneca does something, usually the rest of the colleges follow suit.

True to that text, the following month Georgian College dropped the bomb on everyone's lap just after the students registered for their classes and were getting ready to return to school. It was their own dreadful vaccine mandate that applied to everyone, staff, students, and faculty. I remember reading the first college-wide email from the president, using what I believed to be very aggressive language with phrases like "let me be clear…". I don't particularly like bullies and that's just how I interpreted that language.

I heard that there was going to be a Zoom call sponsored by Children's Health Defense Canada, with a well-known constitutional lawyer named Rocco Galati. There were at least fifteen pages of students and their parents, on that Zoom call.

They were all afraid, and most had never participated in a class-action lawsuit before. Dr. Ponesse and Dr Byram Bridle were also in attendance on that call. Unfortunately, for everyone who attended, the meeting didn't go very well at all, resulting in Rocco Galati yelling at the wonderful woman, from Children's Health Defense Canada, and hanging up from the call. Immediately, Dr. Bridle and a few others started doing damage control and I think somehow, they succeeded.

Now, I don't want this to seem like I'm criticizing Rocco Galati. Just the opposite. In that meeting he stated he hadn't seen his own child in about five months and that he had donated thousands of hours of pro-bono work. He was exhausted and everyone could see that. Many of us understood the reason he was so exhausted, was because he was one of the few courageous lawyers standing up for the rights of too many people against the Covid-19 lunacy happening in this country.

During the meeting, I let it be known I would be willing to be a liaison for Georgian College people, if they were chosen to be part of the class-action lawsuit. Not everyone would be accepted, including me. From that meeting a few people from Georgian reached out to me and we started a small chat group in Telegram with only five of us being Georgian members, but we hoped the group would grow. Ultimately, I don't believe a lawsuit was ever actually filed. I just know I was never part of one.

During one of our five member group meetings during the first week of school, I drafted an email to the president of the college. I decided I would copy as many executives, faculty, and staff as I could, from the internal email system. In total I sent the email to approximately 250 people. It was my hope that I would do two things. One, express my strong objection to the blatant coercion that Georgian College was implementing against people. Two, find more people and let them know that they were not alone and if more people objected, hopefully, management would hear our collective rejection loud and clearly. Wow! Was I ever wrong about the second part!

Being a retired Canadian Military Officer, fortunately I do collect a monthly pension. Without that pension, I could not have afforded to teach at any college because of the exploitive nature of that industry. I was on something called a partial-load contract and I was also mentoring two student projects that were being completed for industry partners. I had hoped to pay my dues as a part-timer, like everyone else, until a spot became available for full-time. So, this meant I was doing the same as a full-time teacher, but for part-time pay. Unfortunately for me, it also put me in the OPSEU union.

The other reason I mentioned the pension was because it made me less financially vulnerable than the other teachers in my chat group, and I felt the prudent thing to do was for them to remain silent partners. I was willing to take the risk, on behalf of the others, simply because I had less financial risk.

Please keep in mind that I am not a lawyer or a retired police officer. However, for months I had been a supporting member of one of the first, most courageous groups of freedom fighters, Police on Guard for Thee, or POG for short. I am not, nor have I been, an admin for POG. I just publicly supported them on their website and was allowed into the Telegram group. I mention them, because in my email to the College, the references to laws came from the Telegram group as an aid we could use, should we need to challenge our employers.

My version was much less detailed than the original, but the intent was similar to the "Notice of Liability" document that was being shared in various groups.

Below is the email I wrote and sent to the 250 plus members of Georgian College.

"Faculty and Staff,

As you are aware, many Colleges and Universities across Ontario, have chosen to institute a Vaccination Mandate. Georgian College has also made the decision to follow this policy with the implementation of Procedures. You may have also heard that there is a Class Action Lawsuit being filed by the Children's Health Defense, represented by the Constitutional Rights Center. As a faculty member I am completely shocked by Georgian College's aggressive stance with these mandates. These mandates contravene:

The Constitution

The Charter of Rights and Freedoms Section 2 (a) and Section 7

The Privacy Act

Ontario Healthcare Consent Act, 1996

Personal Information Protection and Electronic Documents Act, 2000 (PIPEDA)

Personal Health Information Protection Act, 2004 (PHIPA)

Ontario Occupational Health and Safety Act, R. S. O. 1990, c. O. 1

Municipal Freedom of Information and Protection of Privacy Act, RSO 1990.

Bill S – 201, Statues [sic] of Canada 2017: "An Act to prohibit and prevent genetic discrimination."

Nuremberg Code: Article 6: Sections 1 and 3

I am the point of contact for a large, concerned group of Staff and Faculty who feel these mandates are illegal, unjustified, and immoral. If you wish to learn more, please reach out to me on email.

This message has gone to as many faculty and staff as I can reach. Please share this email if you believe Georgian College has exceeded their authority, and the law, by imposing these mandates.

If you feel alone, you are not. There are many of us who believe we must exert our Constitutional Rights against these unlawful measures.

For some of you, this email will come as an enormous relief – reach out to us. For others, it will create anger and frustration. Please keep in mind, this is NOT about Covid-19. This is about the Law and our Human Rights."

Admittedly, I had stretched the truth somewhat when I claimed we were a "large group" because we believed there were many people out there who felt completely alone, but we just hadn't found them yet. This unfortunately, was a completely false assumption.

You see, the line in the last paragraph that says, "For others, it will create anger and frustration", well that was the overwhelming response – anger and frustration towards me.

Within a short time, I received a response from one faculty member saying, "Please remove me from your distribution list." And then, every minute after that, I got people hitting Reply All and saying, "Please remove me from your distribution list." After about the tenth time, one responder said as much as he would love to delete everyone's emails all day long, could everyone just hit reply, and "Please remove me from your distribution list." Then it got even better. One clever, "woke" PhD faculty member actually said something to the effect of, No, I think we should all come out strongly against this person. Within a minute, I was getting hammered with "Please remove me from your distribution list", repeatedly every few seconds to the point where I just shut off my computer for the day. I have to admit, I didn't see that one coming, especially from my supposed friends, my co-ordinator, or the Dean of my faculty.

In terms of the overall attitude of the people on the "distribution list" who supported the vaccine mandates, I was absolutely dumbfounded that these people, who allegedly talk about "critical thinking" with their students, all seemed to lack the basic understanding of how to actually demonstrate critical thinking themselves. It was my naïve belief that all of these "educators" would have been at the forefront of questioning the vaccine mandates; but to my horror, they didn't question them at all. I especially expected a better response after Dr. Ponesse's video had gone viral a few weeks before.

On the bright side, our original group of five did eventually grow by an additional twenty members. A small number, but it was progress and good for our mental health to know there were others listening. Personally, if getting fired for my email gave twenty more people a chance to speak up, it was worth it.

Now, I have to admit something here. I was nervous and my adrenaline was definitely pumping before my finger hit the send button. However, I never waivered. I absolutely never doubted my actions for even a second. That's saying something, especially from someone like me, who has always had reasons to question big decisions. But, in this case, right or wrong, I was absolutely willing to live with the consequences of sending that email. To this very day, I am convinced it was the right thing to do. Furthermore, I could not bear the thought of working for any employer who would so easily violate my rights, without adequate medical justification or respect for the laws in this country. How far, and how easily, would they go if this was allowed to become the standard practice across Canada?

For my efforts, I was fired within a few short days, for "cause". The union was absolutely no help at all. Interestingly, I didn't get fired because I was a bad teacher. In fact my student ratings were always in the 3+ out of 4 range. No probation or slap on the wrist. No counseling. I was fired, because I stood up for myself and I did it in front of 250 people.

As I was being fired in that meeting with the VP of HR, my

email accounts were deleted and I was removed from all the teaching platforms. My two student project members were simply told that I had "moved on" with no explanation to them at all. I was contacted by some students on LinkedIn, and they didn't even know I was no longer teaching at Georgian College. I was erased, and no one noticed.

As of May 2022, I also lost my arbitration, because I was unable to attend the meeting and the arbiter refused to give me a postponement, after she had already given herself two postponements. As a result, I received nothing in terms of what I was seeking. But, again, it was worth taking a stand and I don't regret my actions at all. I will never trade my ethics or values for a paycheck. There are better ways to earn income than to compromise your integrity.

As nice as that sounds, I am fully aware that millions of Canadians were not nearly as fortunate as I was, to be able to make that decision. Millions of Canadians have been forced, or directly coerced, into compromising themselves for the sake of their family's financial security. This, is Canada. These things should have never happened - because it is wrong.

But not all was doom and gloom in society. There were many people who were showing absolute courage and true leadership, especially from members of the policing community. Through my membership in the POG Telegram group, I was able to learn about an outstanding RCMP Officer named Corporal Danny Bulford. He did a Zoom call, which was recorded and later shared, about an investigation he had done regarding Covid-19 vaccinations. At that time, the RCMP had also mandated that all staff would have to take the injection to keep their jobs. Danny said no publicly, which eventually led to him resigning from the RCMP.

There was also another Calgary Senior Police Constable named Brian Denison who resigned and publicly released a video of himself in uniform, recorded in his police cruiser. It was a moment a lot of people had been encouraged by because the police had been a constant disappointment to the public at large, for not standing by the people. They had been extremely aggressive in persecuting Canadians who even dared to question any Covid-19 mandates, especially in cities like Toronto and Calgary. It seemed like the police had turned their backs on the people and didn't think twice about it as long as they continued to get paid their salaries. With the exception of POG members, it had seemed like the police were turning into Nazi Brown Shirts.

There were, at times, other glimmers of hope from the Police, especially when the Convoy was on route to Ottawa. Constable Erin Howard, from the Durham Police Service, did a video supporting the Convoy from her police car while in uniform. Unfortunately for Constable Howard, she was later charged under the Police Services Act. I have to wonder if she would have been charged had she done a video about BLM or some double standard "politically friendly" cause, that her supervisors would have enjoyed. At least with that they could have a demonstration of their social justice brainwashing, being effective on the soft heads of the malleable and complacent police officers.

Conversely, the creation of POG was, in fact, born from the

ethical breaking point for two fiercely courageous Ontario police officers, Constable Chris Vanden Bos and Detective Constable Matt Blacklaws. In December of 2020, two female police officers, in Calgary, arrested a young man for playing outdoor ice hockey and the video of the arrest went viral. For these two patriotic Canadian Police Officers it was the last straw, so they created Police On Guard For Thee, and others immediately joined, including Wendy Long, a retired RCMP Corporal, who has put her heart and soul into the organization since the first week POG was created. She's been at it ever since. These were the people we were waiting on to step up, and they did. Unfortunately, even for them, it's been a difficult battle.

At that time, we still owned a house in Utopia, Ontario. We sold the house in December 2021 and purchased land about three hours away. It all happened quickly, and we almost ended up living in a hotel for the winter.

Fortunately, one night I had driven past the motel we had booked and the parking lot was full of police cars. It turned out to be some sort of police raid, and it wasn't the first time it happened. Not wanting to subject our five-year-old to that, we immediately looked for a more secure place to live. Luckily, we found an apartment, last minute and moved in right away and put half of our things in storage. I was waiting for January 1, 2022, to cash an RRSP to live on, while we built the house that year. I didn't know it at the time, but my life was about to change course, both dramatically and quickly.

Chapter 1

A Friend of a Friend

When we moved, my daughter's mother answered a Facebook post to get our now six-year-old, together with some like-minded people and their daughter for a playdate. That's how we met Joe, Wendy, and Violet.

Joe and I really hit it off and during our conversation, he told me his friend Jane Moffat had been doing crypto for a few years. I asked him if he would be willing to introduce me to Jane so I could learn more about Crypto, to see if there was a way to earn some passive income. I didn't want to get scammed by some online crypto guru, and I wanted to meet a real person who was not trying to sell me garbage. To my surprise, Jane had me over the following week and we spent three hours talking about many different things, including Crypto. Even though that meeting was very informative, I decided to forgo investing in Cryptocurrency for the time being.

In early January, I heard about the Trucker Convoy that was heading to Ottawa to protest all of the government-imposed mandates. I was absolutely intrigued by the idea and was thrilled that someone had thought of something so brilliant.

Before I went back to school to do my software degree, I retired from the Canadian Army in 2015. I had joined the Infantry, as a reservist, in February of 1990 when I was only sixteen years old but because I was in my seventeenth year, I was allowed to join early. In 1997, I graduated from Niagara College in Construction Engineering Technology and Architecture. I supported myself in those days, working for the Army, doing odd jobs, and with student loans. In 1996, I was on a course called Assault Pioneer, which is the Infantry version of a basic Combat Engineer. I mention this course because that was when I met a brilliant man named James Topp. He was a Regular Force Army Corporal, and I was a Reserve Corporal. James is an incredibly smart man, and I've often wondered if he has a photographic memory because he is the type of guy who studies twenty minutes and always seems to get 100% on his tests. He was even the top student on that course. James and I hit it off. Over the years we didn't have much contact with each other, but in the military that's just how it goes, though you make friends for life with people you train with. If you don't know who James Topp is, he is a Warrant Officer who started CanadaMarches.ca and completed a walk across Canada from the Terry Fox statue in Vancouver, BC to Ottawa. The journey started on February 20, 2022 and ended at the Tomb of the Unknown Soldier, in Ottawa on June 30, 2022. The trip took 131 days, and he walked over 4,300 km/2,672 mi. More about James Topp later!

In 1998, I enrolled in the Regular Force Army, as a Combat Engineer Officer. During my time as a Regular Force member, I missed out on multiple tours overseas, but it wasn't for lack of trying. In 2008, I was a day away from starting the pre-deployment training for Afghanistan when my boss informed me that our social worker recommended, I didn't go. My son would be having his second open heart surgery sometime after the deployment to Afghanistan, so it was considered too much of a risk of becoming an administrative burden to the military.

What was particularly frustrating was that I was already on something called IR, or Imposed Restriction, meaning I lived in another city during the work week anyway. My son had all the support he could need. I still wasn't living with him and his mother but was prevented from deploying. This is where jokes about military intelligence are appropriate. In truth, it seemed to me that my new boss just didn't want to be understaffed and was looking for a reason to keep me or anyone else from leaving.

I did however, work as a duty officer, on the G8/G20 Summit in Toronto in 2010. To be clear, I was of no significance to this particular tasking and was in fact the night-time duty officer, where nothing ever happened. I'll come back to this point soon because there is a reason why I mentioned it!

Of all the training and experiences I've ever had, I will say that the one course I did, that will have a lasting impact on me was the Army Operations Course, or AOC. I completed that course in December of 2007, and it was the thirteenth serial that had run since it was re-created as AOC. The course was approximately six months long and was taught at the Command and Staff College in Kingston Ontario. It deals with battle planning at the Operational Level, which for the Army is up to a brigade. By far, it was my favorite course in my military career. What you learn there is a mile wide in terms of knowledge, but you only have time to absorb about one inch deep. I wasn't there to become the top candidate; I was just there to learn as much as I could.

During the beginning of the pandemic, I believed from day one that this was not at all what it appeared to be. However, for the sake of my family, in particular my son, I was still extremely cautious. In fact, I didn't go see my son from the time of the lockdowns, until his birthday in May.

I had never missed his birthday, and I wasn't going to miss this one. I drove to see him and stayed outside in his front yard, in the cold rain under an umbrella and blanket for most of the day. I saw him on his birthday, and that was what was important. In fact, with my kids, it's not technically their birthday until the exact moment of their birth, so I was with my son until exactly 6:26 PM so I could wish him a happy birthday in person. The hardest part was not being able to give him a hug or have any contact with him at all.

As time when on, I started to question the official government narratives about Covid-19. I remember telling an Army friend, who absolutely doubted my sanity, that something was wrong, I just didn't know what. And therein lies the challenge. I didn't know who my adversary was, or what their capabilities were, or the weapons they were using. It wasn't like doing an Intelligence Preparation of the Battlefield (IPB) against the German Army in WW2. It was an unknown adversary, with unknown capabilities or a stated declaration of their intent. It was incredibly frustrating to not be able to conduct my own Operational Planning Process (OPP) to protect my family. While I had prepared, the scenarios were too vast to plan for everything.

When I first heard about the Freedom Convoy, heading toward Ottawa, I knew it was going to be a game changer. I just didn't know I would have anything to do with it.

It was AOC that prepared me the most technically, for what I would need for the Freedom Convoy in January of 2022. However, nothing could have prepared me on a personal level, for what was to come.

Chapter 2

From Pancakes to the Convoy

As I mentioned earlier, I was not involved in the planning or creation of the Convoy, and I didn't know who was. I knew the trucks would be passing by my area at different times during the last week in January, so on Thursday, the 27th I called my new friend Joe and asked him if he wanted to go waive at the Convoy passing by our area on the 401 Highway. As it happened, Joe had spent all week planning for approximately 175 trucks to stop at his place overnight. He had several acres of his land plowed, with port-a-potties, lights, and a massive amount of hot food at his place to take care of them for the night. I offered to come over and help him and he accepted.

To say that Joe was frustrated, would be an understatement. Mostly because of the challenges of dealing with local government officials who were not too happy that he was helping the Convoy. In fact, they went so far as to put concrete barriers on his road, stating that the tiny bridge there wouldn't stand up to all those trucks. One of Joe's neighbors sorted that out, citing medical risks for her father and that the road could not be blocked for emergency services if needed.

When I arrived at Joe's, everything was well in hand, except there were no trucks yet. We waited, and after several hours, heard there was an accident on the 401 Highway and that the police had been rerouting the trucks around Joe's exit, so there was a risk they would miss his place entirely. Joe had been on the phone constantly, dealing with many people in the Convoy, but his frustration just seemed to compound.

At one point, I spoke to Joe and told him I would stay there and help if the trucks arrived. During that conversation, I also learned that our friend Jane was the one who got Joe involved because she had dealings with James Bauder from Canada Unity. At that time, I had never heard of Canada Unity or James Bauder. Joe told me that earlier in the week, he recommended to Jane to get me involved because they both knew I was a retired army officer and could probably handle the logistics of much of this easily.

Unfortunately, the issue with the highway accident wasn't

going away, so Joe and I started planning a way to put guides on each corner of the route to his land. By that time, it was late in the evening, and we just didn't have enough volunteers left to cover every corner. So, I went out on my own and planted myself in the middle of a traffic circle, with a headlamp on, trying to signal the Convoy and direct them toward Joe's. This too was problematic because, although trucks were going past me on the traffic circle, I didn't know which was a Convoy truck, or which was a truck just doing its route. I had no way of knowing and couldn't stop the steady flow of trucks going around the circle or I'd risk an accident or traffic jam.

At about 1:00 a.m. I was ready to pack it in, when Andrea, another volunteer, arrived to see if we could figure something out. By 1:30 a.m. there was no more traffic at all, so I assumed the highway was now clear. We decided to go home and by 2:00 a.m. I was back at the apartment.

I spoke to Joe the next day and he told me the trucks stopped for the night at an On Route near Kingston and that some of the first trucks had already made their way into Ottawa on Friday morning. It was an incredibly frustrating and disappointing result for everyone, especially Joe who had put that much effort into helping the Convoy.

---

30 January 2022

Two days later on Sunday morning, the 30th of January, I was still in my PJs and making pancakes with my daughter. I had just gotten off a call with Chris Vanden Bos, because I saw a video he did while taking his family to Ottawa. It was of him in his vehicle, filming all the people waving flags on the highway overpasses, along his journey. It was an incredibly emotional and inspiring video, that he shared with everyone.

At about 11 a.m. I received a call from Jane. We went through the normal pleasantries and then she asked me if I would be willing to have a call with a Convoy organizer named James Bauder and his wife Sandy. They wanted to talk about planning and logistics, now that the Convoy had arrived in Ottawa and had been there for almost two days. I was more than happy to take that call with the hopes I could give them some good advice to make things go smoothly while they were there. That seemed to be what they were looking for.

A few minutes later I was on a call with Jane and Sandy, but James was delayed and joined in a few minutes. When James arrived on the call we immediately started to talk about the current situation and then James wanted to know about my qualifications and experiences with the army. I briefly mentioned my experience on the G8/G20 Summit in Toronto in 2010, because it pertained to working with the police, which is what the Convoy organizers would need to do. Now, remember, I was only the night shift duty officer during the Summit, not the planner or leader. There was a Brigadier General in Charge, not Captain Tom Marazzo. I think the call lasted about fifteen minutes total, and the end result was that James asked me if I could come to Ottawa for a few days to help out.

As we were talking, I left my daughter and walked down the hall to where her mother was working at her desk. I whispered and made some hand gestures, that I was asked to go to Ottawa. She got up from her desk and started packing me a bag of clothes and some food – enough for 5 days. When I hung up the phone, we had a quick chat about what was happening and what I'd be doing. I had a shower, got dressed, and started packing the car. For some reason, my daughter's mother also prepared my suit and had it ready to go. I asked her why because I didn't think I'd need it for any possible reason. She just looked at me and said, "Take it, Trust me." I have to admit, I was a little embarrassed about the comment, but I wasn't sure why and ultimately, I never did end up wearing it.

As soon as I started the drive toward Ottawa, I received a call from an unknown number, so I assumed it was either from James or Sandy again. It turned out to be Chris Vanden Bos calling from his wife's phone. James asked him to touch base with me, not knowing that Chris and I had already known each other for a long time. I was encouraged by the fact that many great organizations were coming together in Ottawa to stand side-by-side against Trudeau's ridiculous and illogical mandates.

Within three hours of that initial phone call with James and Sandy, I was in Ottawa looking for the Arc Hotel. I had gone north, up Bank Street, but Bank was completely blocked by trucks past Laurier Avenue. I wondered if we were waiting for a light or if it had been completely blocked off by trucks. It turned out it was blocked, and I was concerned because cars were starting to block me in from behind as well. It was complete chaos on that corner, and I wondered what the rest of the city was like too. I couldn't imagine driving a truck in that mess.

Eventually, the people behind me realized the same thing so they backed up and left and I did the same thing, looking for a place to park my car. I ended up parking on Gloucester Street for the time being until I knew where I was going to be staying for the night. I just hoped that I wouldn't get towed, ticketed, or both.

As I was walking, I couldn't believe how cold it was. I only had to go two blocks and even though I was completely dry it felt like my pants were damp and sticking to my skin. I had lived in Petawawa, Ontario and Gagetown, New Brunswick, so cold temperatures were nothing new to me, but the feeling of that cold was something I'd never experienced before.

At approximately 2:30 p.m. I finally arrived in the lobby of the Arc Hotel. It was buzzing with a lot of activity. I had no idea what James or Sandy looked like so I texted James to let him know I was the *business casual* guy who was out of place amongst the Truckers in the lobby. James came out of the conference room and immediately recognized me when he saw how I was dressed. We didn't have time for chit-chat, and he ushered me into the conference room ahead of him.

The room was full of people sitting around a huge conference table. Two Ottawa police Sergeants were also there at the opposite end of the table. This was my first introduction to Sgt. Phong Le and Sgt. Louis Carvello, part of the Police Liaison Team.

As James and I walked into the room, Sgt. Carvello asked me to either take my phone outside or turn it off. I turned it off, for the moment. While I was dealing with my phone, James introduced me to the room.

Now, I cannot be sure of the exact words James used, but it was something to the effect of, "This is Tom. He's a retired army officer and he ran the G8/G20 Summit in 2010 and he's here to take charge of all our logistics while we're in Ottawa." I'm absolutely certain, that's not exactly what he said, but it was most definitely the sentiment that registered in my brain after he had spoken. For the most part, I had the expectation that I would just spend a few days there, get everything organized with a good sustainment plan, then hand it off to someone else. Honestly, that's what I was expecting to do. Was I ever wrong!

As I sat at the table, Sgt. Carvello asked me for my name and phone number. As he was writing, one of the Truckers said they were surprised I gave them my name. I replied, "I put my name on everything I do."

At that point, the meeting with the others had already started and since I didn't know anyone in the room, except for James, I decided to just observe and try to assess the people who were there. There were some very intense moments between the police and the Convoy people. I was somewhat surprised because it left me with the feeling that after two days of being in Ottawa, it was the first time they had all sat down for a meeting together. From my observations, the two Officers were not making a very good impression on anyone, and they didn't seem to listen nearly as much as they liked to speak.

During my time in the army, I completed my MBA, part-time over several years. I focused my electives on negotiations and influence, so I understand the vocabulary and structure of a negotiation extremely well. As a side note, I have a perverse love of negotiating new vehicles because its as hard a negotiation as any and is great practice. So, I was expecting a dialogue with the police in an initial meeting, not the demand for solutions off the top. They seemed impatient and keen to get down to business. They did very little to build trust with us and seemed to focus on their demands, instead of listening and building a rapport.

Fortunately for me, there was an empty seat beside an incredible woman named Dana Metcalfe. Dana is an absolutely beautiful woman, with a brilliant mind for - well everything. She is incredibly strong with social media, event planning, and organizing. As soon as I spoke to her, I knew she was not to be underestimated and would be someone I was going to work with, very well.

Across the table from me was and another amazing human being named Ryan Olson. Ryan was someone who I was absolutely sure I had recognized from a social media video. After the meeting, Ryan and I had a chance to talk, and he thought he had seen me before too. It turns out, there was no possible way for us to have known each other, especially since he was there, all the way from Saskatchewan. Ryan is one of those people who is young but with about 100 years of experience. I can't remember when it was exactly but I started referring to him as *Baby Face Ryan*, because it just baffled me how someone so young, could be so experienced at reading a room of strangers. Ryan was seated beside his father-in-law, Joseph Bourgault, who in 2022 was vying to become the leader of the Federal Conservative Party. It wasn't until I was home from Ottawa that I learned Joe was the father of Ryan's wife. There were other special people in the meeting as well.

In the early days of the Convoy, Dana was essential to building our safety plan to keep the roads open to EMS vehicles. Working with Dana was always great. At the time, I didn't know what her role was from the Newfoundland Convoy. I certainly wasn't going to admit to anyone that I didn't know who the key players were. None of these people knew who I was either, so I had to make sure I didn't cause any doubts about my capabilities to help, by inadvertently insulting someone who I should have known due to their notoriety. Another person I met was Leanne Carter. Leanne has a way of looking at you to show she's listening, but you can tell her mind is going a mile a minute.

Another hard-working man I met was Mike Stack. A great guy, who gave his heart and soul to everything he did during the Convoy. He would become instrumental in liaising with OPS and also being my eyes out on the streets.

There were a lot of people in that room, and since it was the first time, I had ever met any of them, I can't recall everyone who was there. As I was sitting there quietly, listening for the meeting to conclude, a finger pointed from across the room that stopped everyone from leaving. Rick Sproull, who turned out to be another really great person, just said, "I want to hear what he has to say." Honestly, my first thought was that I just wanted to know where I was going to be sleeping for the next few days, and what came out of my mouth was some quick-thinking song and dance about needing to assess the situation and go from there. Again, I didn't know anyone, and it was vital that I maintain any perceived level of competence and credibility if I was going to be able to help everyone get a sustainment plan organized.

Even from that initial meeting, I could see there wasn't a specific person who was the obvious leader of the Convoy. It was very organic. It reminded me of the joke about the old Sea King helicopters that flew on our Naval Frigates. The joke is that they are 10,000 individual parts, flying in unison. So far, I had the feeling this Convoy was doing the same thing – but that's by no means a criticism because it was an advantage for us that I wanted to maintain into the future. What I immediately realized was that this was very different from my army days because back then, subordinates were legally bound to follow my orders. With the Truckers, I wasn't signing anyone's paycheck, nor did I have delegated authority over them to give orders. No one had any obligation to listen to me and this was going to be entirely about developing their trust in me, using nothing but interpersonal skills and sound decision-making. Building and maintaining credibility is vital for anyone assuming a leadership role, especially from someone who wasn't a Trucker!

The best thing I had going for me was that James Bauder had, on his own, dramatically oversold my involvement at the G8/G20 Summit and my role in the army in general. In the future, I did set the record straight about the Summit with people. Admittedly, that first impression did give me some instant credibility, so I wasn't going to change that perception about myself to the group at that point.

The meeting finally concluded, and once I spoke to Ryan and found a place to sleep, I immediately started getting to work figuring out where everyone was and how many vehicles we had. This would turn out to be a much harder challenge than I ever anticipated.

Chapter 3

Situational Awareness

The very first thing that needed to happen was for me to look at a map and find out where everyone was located. The challenge was that I had spent very little time in Ottawa, so I didn't know the terrain. In the Army, we do something called *Christening of the Ground* and it's meant for those who are receiving orders, to get something called SA, or Situational Awareness. In my case there was no map, therefore, no Christening of the Ground, and I would have to develop my own SA from conversations I would have with people who didn't know where anything was either.

The good news was, in an almost cartoon-like fashion, a

talented guy named Andrew Peloso, arrived with two large-scale maps of the area we were operating in. Andrew and his friend Jeremy Regoto drove from Alberta to Ottawa, as a last-minute dare to start filming everything with the hopes of making a documentary. As they drove to Ottawa, they literally created their website, www.TruckingForFreedom.com, in the car. The documentary is also called Trucking for Freedom. They are co-directors and successfully crowdfunded for the film very quickly. During their time in Ottawa, their team grew, adding Carrera Banman and Matt Robar to start capturing as much footage as possible. They had also put out a call to the public to share whatever footage they shot, to their website.

Initially, I had no idea who they were or what their purpose was, but what I quickly realized was they were doing extremely important work and they were there to tell Canadians the truth about what the mainstream media was already lying about daily regarding the Convoy.

I had been told there was a small map floating around and that there was an agreement between the Ottawa Police Service or OPS, for where the trucks could park. What I found out later was when this plan was approved by the OPS, it was under the assumption that the Convoy would only be there for approximately three days. Oops! Nevertheless, we started to transfer some of the information we had from the small map, onto the large map that was covering our table. Many of the people there had no idea who I was, other than from what James had said when he originally introduced me, but I immediately knew they were incredibly strong-willed and highly capable team players.

I discussed some of the people we encountered while having a conversation with Leanne and Dana, while we were working on the map. What I didn't find out until weeks later, was how the original idea for the Freedom Convoy came to be. I was told a female trucker had an incredibly horrific encounter with the Canadian Border Services Agency (CBSA) as she re-entered Canada. Upon re-entering, she was removed from her truck by three CBSA agents, detained, and badly treated. She was mentally and physically abused for having the audacity to do her job, in Canada, as an unvaccinated truck driver. Ironically, months before, Justin Trudeau was publicly applauding Truckers. But without proof of vaccine, they had been deemed a threat to public safety and now needed to quarantine for fourteen days, upon returning to Canada. This non-scientific dictate made it impossible for Truckers to do their jobs. It was from that incident involving this one truck driver and the CBSA, that the idea for the Freedom Convoy came into existence.

One of the things I wanted to impress upon everyone working on the map was if we were going to be there for a long time, we had to become partners with the OPS. We needed to work with them, not against them.

There are other Police agencies in Ottawa as well. There's the Parliamentary Protective Service, or PPS, who has jurisdiction around Parliament Hill. There is also the RCMP and the OPP. What was interesting to us was that we would later learn, there was confusion between the OPS and the PPS, as to where the jurisdictional boundary was on Wellington. If we couldn't develop a good relationship with the police, it would only make our time in Ottawa even more difficult than it already was, while surviving in a cold vehicle in freezing -25C/-13F temperatures.

Additionally, we had to focus our efforts on being safe and responsible in terms of keeping unencumbered access to emergency services anywhere we were located. This was of paramount importance to me, and I had to impress upon the Truckers that it needed to become vital to them too. If one person anywhere, could not receive emergency services because of us, we would be in real trouble, and from my perspective it would be unforgivable.

So, the first thing we plotted on the map were the locations of vulnerable places, like hospitals, long-term care homes, fire and police stations, etc. We then looked at the highspeed routes to the hospitals. Once we had those places clearly marked, we then compared their locations to the routes the OPS had asked us not to be on.

From my brief walk to the Arc Hotel, I realized that Ottawa is one of those cities with lots of confusing one-way streets. Often one-way streets were three lanes wide, so that was good for us in terms of safety lanes. I asked, not demanded, that we keep at least one lane open on every street we were parked on and as a general rule, that we stay off any single-lane street. I didn't believe there was such a thing, but I wanted to strongly convey safety, so I exaggerated the point by talking about non-existent single-lane streets. If we were on a two-lane street, we needed to keep one lane open. If we were on a three-lane street, I asked to keep one of the outside lanes open. However, one of the Truckers suggested that we keep the center lane open because it would make it safer for vehicles when they approached an intersection and tried to make a turn in either direction. In my experience, sometimes people will become defiant of sound logic, just because they don't like the person who presented the idea, so I was always careful not to "give orders", but rather make a compelling case for everyone to buy into.

Since I didn't know everyone, I was focused on building relationships with people. One thing that I did on my first day, was to ask Jane Moffat if she would also come to Ottawa. She arrived with Andrea, who a few nights before, was standing on the traffic circle with me in the freezing cold. I asked Jane to come to Ottawa because I didn't know any of the other people and she did. Unfortunately, they only stayed that afternoon and returned home that night. Before Jane left, she mentioned to me that when it came to James, I would sometimes need to focus him on one issue at a time because he was prone to taking on too many things at once. Unfortunately, after meeting a few dozen people that day, and two others named James as well, I later lost track of which James she was referring to.

I realized immediately that there were a lot of strong personalities, and with strong personalities come big egos! In the Army, you can counter a strong ego when people fall under your direct command or supervision. When you are the delegated authority, you are responsible for everything your subordinates do. In that context, your responsibility as the leader is to make decisions. Interestingly, when you are legitimately in charge of people, you can delegate your authority to a subordinate to act on your behalf. However, you cannot delegate your responsibility for the actions your subordinates take on your behalf. In my case, I had no legitimate or delegated authority. No one did at that point. If I was going to be effective, I had to earn trust, and quickly.

While I realized I was being scrutinized by everyone, I was also trying to figure out who the "alphas" were. Not just the alphas. I was looking for the alphas who could deliver. For this, I had to be extremely patient. In truth, it took me about three days to figure out who were the alpha "talkers" and who were the alpha "doers".

Once we finished marking all of the vulnerable infrastructure on the map, we needed to learn how many trucks we had, where they were, and the types of vehicles. This would be an absolutely monumental task and to my dismay and frustration, it took four days to figure it all out. One of the reasons was that some Convoys, who had been there from day one, had departed the city to go back to work. Simultaneously, new Convoys were arriving each day. You would think it would be an easy task to count trucks and people, given that when a regional convoy left their hometown from each province, they would know their numbers. That was certainly true during the drive to Ottawa. However, once the convoys from all over Canada started arriving in Ottawa, many of the groups got separated upon entering the city. There was a lot of confusion, which was caused by the OPS and the lack of planning by some of the designated convoy organizers themselves. Upon immediate arrival, the Truckers didn't know where the trucks could and could not go. It had the unfortunate effect of scattering individual trucks all over the city, separating them from their original convoy. This was something that happened before my arrival, so I could not influence that phase of the trip, but I had to make the best of it. Once the trucks had descended on Ottawa, the OPS started erecting blockades on many of the roads. This meant that once the trucks initially stopped, there was very little room to maneuver on a street, let alone move a packet of vehicles to another section of the city to link up with the original convoy they left home with. The end result was that many convoys traveled to Ottawa, but then they got scattered all over the downtown area. One of the concepts we came up with was to designate a "Block Captain" to look after their city block. This would be successful, only so long as individual Truckers would use their own initiative and seek and accept responsibility for their blocks. Many did, but the lines of communication, from each Block Captain and the Arc Hotel, were extremely weak. This was something that would later come back to bite me in the ass, repeatedly, for days.

In those first few days, the closest analogy I could use to describe my personal situation is that of getting a battlefield promotion several ranks up and becoming a Brigade Commander while getting dropped into an ongoing battle, having never met any subordinate Commanders, not knowing what vehicles were in the fight, or where they were. Nor did I have an appreciation of their capabilities, while simultaneously having no reliable means of communication with the troops. All of this, with nothing but a vague mission statement to end all federal mandates.

In truth, what I walked into was incredibly difficult, and as patient as I wanted to be, the Convoy was already in Ottawa. I had to influence decisions very quickly because there didn't appear to be any clearly defined leadership among the Truckers out in the streets. There were the original Convoy organizers, but in terms of my perception, who was running things now that the Truckers were in Ottawa? This was having a very negative impact on morale, and rumors of Truckers getting angry and ready to leave were starting to surface after only three days.

That first day was a whirlwind of meeting new people. Most I didn't know, but two I'd definitely seen before. I had finally found my hotel room and was heading back into the conference room when I saw someone I recognized. I was embarrassed to admit I couldn't remember his name, but I knew immediately who he was from the video he did with POG. It was Corporal Danny Bulford, the former RCMP officer. As I introduced myself, and thanked him for everything he had done, I realized the person he was talking to was Brian Dennison, the Calgary Police Officer who had also resigned on a video in his police car, after twenty-four years of police service. It was extremely humbling to be able to thank these two courageous men, for sacrificing so much for the public. I was honored to meet them, but instead of embarrassing myself, I made jokes about how much taller they both looked on video, to which they both agreed. I didn't know it at the time, but this was the first of many introductions to people who I would come to recognize as courageous freedom fighters in Canada.

During the first day, I kept hearing about a few people, two in particular - Tamara and Chris. I didn't know who they were, and I couldn't ask anyone yet. I just knew they were important and very likely the main leaders. As it turned out, they were definitely key players, and for good reason. I was told later that Tamara would be coming to the Arc Hotel. That evening she arrived and brought Thomas O'Connor with her. During that initial meeting, I didn't get to talk to Tamara privately. We just went through the typical tactical training of some kind. You just know it when you see it and as it turned out, he was a former Paramedic with the City of Ottawa. He was also a tactical medic on the OPS team. So, he had specialist tactical training and a lot of experience doing his job in a high-risk situation involving the police.

Thomas is one of those people who is also respectfully blunt. Although he had no idea who I was, one of the first things he said to me was that by allowing the trucks to be stationary, I was making a huge tactical mistake, especially given his experience working with the OPS. His rationale was that while the trucks remained stationary, the police would slowly start to restrict their movements with barriers while simultaneously planning for mass arrests. Basically, the longer we were there and not moving, the easier it would be for them to execute their plans in the future if we did not leave. He recommended that we remain constantly mobile in some areas, to counter their ability to plan.

As much as I understood Thomas' rationale, by that time I already knew it was going to be impossible to remain constantly mobile. We couldn't get organized while parked, so becoming mobile would have been dangerous. We risked not being able to maintain a presence in the downtown area because the police would simply have put-up barriers. However, what Thomas said was true and it would factor into much of our future planning. I just didn't believe we could pull it off without shooting ourselves in the foot. From a military doctrine perspective, one thing that we could do is hold and maintain ground. For the time being, our best course of action would be to hold the ground, on Wellington and the perpendicular streets, as much as possible,

It was during this meeting with Tamara and Thomas that I learned there was another HQ set up in a completely different hotel called The Swiss. This was interesting to me because if there was a leadership vacuum at the Arc Hotel, why was there another HQ, instead of everyone being under the same roof? What was explained to me, in that meeting, was that the Arc Hotel would be completely responsible for everything involving Trucker movement, food, and fuel. The Swiss Hotel would handle medical and security as well as the stage that was used for public speaking events with VIPs.

I was just happy to get a further reduction on our list of responsibilities. The one thing that Thomas and I had agreed to do was keep in constant communication. I planned to go visit the Swiss Hotel in the morning, to see for myself what they had going on and to meet their team.

It was the first day and already getting extremely late, so I decided to find my room, which had finally been taken care of by Ryan Olsen. That would be one of four different hotel rooms I would be in during my time in Ottawa, but in typical Army fashion, I always had my kit ready to move at a moment's notice.

---

31 January 2022

The next morning, I decided to do a recce, or reconnaissance, of the Swiss Hotel. The Swiss was about a 1.5 km/1 mi walk from the Arc Hotel and I actually enjoyed getting out and seeing what was going on in the streets. What was bizarre to me was to get to the Arc Hotel, I had to walk past the Canadian Armed Force's former National Defence Head Quarters. It was the representation of the building and its use that had an impact on me. I just hoped our Convoy would not see a situation where the Canadian Military would get involved.

As I arrived at the Swiss, I was immediately envious that they had a secured front door, with a doorbell camera on it. I had to ring to get in. It wasn't like that at the Arc Hotel at all. The Arc was a free-for-all. After several tries, a woman came to the door and let me in. As she took me to the basement level, I was immediately impressed by the kitchen area and the fact that people were getting organized for the day. There was already a closed-door meeting in progress, so I would have to wait until Thomas came out to get me.

While I waited, I made a coffee and met a guy I came to refer to as John Fuel. He was seated at a table with another person, and they were busy planning some logistical fuel issues. So, "Fuel" for obvious reasons.

The meeting ended and I was introduced to some of the Swiss Hotel team members. Danny Bulford was in there as well and I learned he would be working out of there on security.

From my perspective, they had an almost proper Operations Center set up. They had radios, laptops, whiteboards, maps, and lots of spreadsheets going. I was far behind them in my setup, but that's why I was brought in to begin with. I had to admit, I was still a little surprised there were two different HQs, and I thought they should have been combined into one. However, redundancy was also helpful, and as time passed, it was obvious they wouldn't have been able to work in such close proximity without causing too much chaos.

After a few hours at the Swiss, I learned what I needed to know and decided to head back to the Arc Hotel. The front lobby was a hive of activity, and again I wished we had a locked and secured front entrance like the Swiss. One thing that was absolutely clear to me was that most of the people in the lobby of the Arc Hotel didn't need to be there. They were looking for information about what was happening. That was fair, given they had been sitting in their trucks for three full days, after driving across the country for over a week. They just wanted some direction.

As I entered our conference room, there were people going in and out as well. They were mostly trying to figure out what to do next, but without a central person or team, there was a natural hesitancy to make decisions. I decided to call a meeting to see where everyone was at, in terms of what information they could provide to the group.

This probably has to go on record as the most unproductive meeting I've ever participated in, in terms of getting work done – however, it turned out to be a very revealing meeting. I don't remember all the original participants of this meeting, but I do recall Dana Metcalfe and Leanne Carter being there with people who were shaping up to be a core group during that first week.

The meeting had just begun when the door opened, and in came three men and a woman. I had no idea who they were, but we informed them we were starting a meeting and to please wait outside. They very politely refused, and I turned on my diplomacy switch because I legitimately wanted to hear what they were so upset about. Yes, they were upset!

What was immediately apparent was that this group arrived in Ottawa together and were godly people. They were frustrated with the current situation because they were just sitting in their trucks, and no one was telling them anything. They had other grievances too, but this was the main issue, and it was when I first realized that discontentment was spreading across the Convoy.

Comprehending that part of the conversation was quick and very informative. What came next was altogether different. This was my first experience within the Convoy, with the power of faith leading Canadians to be in Ottawa. Our new friends were adamant that they were drawn to Ottawa, because of God. This was both fascinating and unexpected, but welcome.

In my life, I have always struggled with the concept of religious doctrine versus being a spiritual person. Like everyone else, I've suffered my own life challenges, and in that area, my stories are nothing special. I've always been very envious of the "faith" people have in God through religion because during the most difficult moments of a person's life, they have the emotional support they need to endure almost anything.

At this meeting, I realized I was surrounded by many exceptional people who are Christians, and someone asked that we pray before the start of every meeting. I certainly did not view it as a "request" as I didn't see it as something I had the right to overrule just because I was chairing the meeting. The people at that table derived an enormous amount of strength from God, and I was never going to interfere with something so personal or powerful to each of them.

As the meeting with our new guests continued, the tone started to take a very awkward and unproductive turn, when the woman felt the need to pray for Dana and save her from her wicked ways. Dana wanted nothing to do with that conversation and at one point asked the woman to remove her hand from Dana's arm in a very polite but assertive way. To this day, it is still unclear to me what the exact nature of these four people's grievances were, other than not enough information being passed to the individual Truckers.

I'm not relating this story as a means of making fun of anyone I mention it because that was when I discovered how strong Dana is, while simultaneously realizing we were going to be a lightning rod for some incredibly bizarre situations. In both cases, I was right.

As a side note, that evening I discovered one of our people, Tehan, had been sleeping on the floor in the lobby of the Arc Hotel for two nights. I offered him my hotel room key so he could have a good night's sleep and take a shower. He reluctantly took the key. I figured I'd find somewhere else to sleep, which I did. The next morning, I had to go to my room to get something, only to find the woman who wanted to save Dana's soul at our meeting the day before, sleeping in the bed with her husband while Tehan slept on the floor beside them. Every day I saw examples of this type of self-sacrifice and kindness, from people like Tehan. I was surrounded by Canadians who gave so much of themselves for the sake of their children, family, and communities.

The night after I met Tamara, I met Chris Barber. It was a very similar meeting to when I met Tamara and Thomas. When you first meet Chris, what is most striking about him is how big he actually is. He's 6'4" and 260 pounds, and his personality is just as large, but in a totally disarming and charismatic way. Despite his size, he has this unique way of making you feel like you're talking to your best friend from childhood. Chris sometimes describes himself as a "troll" on TikTok, but in reality, he's actually a "counter-troll" and only makes fun of people who troll him first. But, in typical Chris Barber fashion, he does it in a very funny and friendly way, as if you're being made fun of by one of your buddies. He's definitely not a pushover either, but he lives by a code. Chris is a guy who will meet any challenger of a fight, but then go buy them a beer, after kicking their ass.

I remember initially hearing Chris wasn't feeling well and was resting in his hotel room for most of the day, which was why we planned to meet in the evening. He came into the Arc Hotel conference room, with his hoodie up over his head and was practically hugging a hot coffee cup. He looked as rough as he felt. Someone in the room introduced us and as we shook hands, my first thought was "Crap, I'm going to regret that," as I certainly didn't want whatever he had. I did sanitize my hand, but it was too late and that was the moment I was simultaneously introduced to the Omicron variant of Covid-19.

Unfortunately, it took me several days to realize it was Covid but to be perfectly honest, I didn't care if it was Covid or just some other respiratory illness I've had at various times throughout my life. I was later told it was likely Omicron, by two of the doctors who frequented the Arc Hotel and was put on one of the Covid-19 protocols of Ivermectin, Aspirin, and vitamins.

I knew my chances of surviving Covid at the time, was 99.97%. If Canadian citizens didn't stand up for their Rights, we would have had almost a 100% chance of being completely removed from Canadian society, so I wasn't going to let a chest cold remove me from what needed to be done for the sake of my children.

For the remainder of my time in Ottawa, I dealt with an incredibly annoying chest cold, and that was all the attention I was willing to give it. Miraculously, I survived Covid-19.

Chapter 4

Wellington, Morale, and Media

What I immediately realized on day one, was that the entire Convoy was lacking a unifying plan where individuals could use their own initiative to guide their daily decisions. Without it, I knew this was going to rapidly lead to a decline in morale and our sense of cohesion. They needed a tangible focus, not an abstract mission statement that wasn't prescriptive in a way that would help them end the federal mandates, especially from their trucks.

For this, I started developing three specific priorities, but it would take me a few days to formulate them properly. I specifically wanted only three because they would be easy to remember and easier to focus people's efforts on. Once I finalized them, I would do my best to communicate them to those people I considered influential leaders. In a sense, I was trying to convey an intent, so that leaders at the lowest level could become self-directed toward achieving my priorities. Each priority also needed to reinforce the other two, but there was most certainly an order of operation for each priority to strengthen the others.

The first priority and most obvious to everyone was Wellington Street, right in front of Parliament Hill. Several months after the Convoy ended, this priority would become highly controversial amongst several Convoy participants that don't understand tactics, negotiations, or diplomacy. However, during the Convoy it was a generally understood and accepted priority that most people understood.

Clearly, from an optics point of view, we had to have as much of Wellington as we could get. It was absolutely critical that we had as many vehicles on that street as possible. I wasn't thinking about the tactics of being on Wellington. I was considering what the public would see from a camera lens when watching the Convoy from a screen. I remembered watching a documentary where John Perkins, the author of "Confessions of an Economic Hitman" was interviewed. He was reflecting on the idea that if you showed approximately a thousand people protesting through a camera lens, the viewers at home got the impression that it was the entire country protesting. I really wanted the Canadian public to feel like there were a million supportive Canadians who went to Ottawa to end the mandates too. People will naturally gravitate toward the majority group, and I wanted them to at least reflect on why the Convoy was in Ottawa. They will get behind a cause, especially if they feel like they're missing out on the next big thing. The perception of a million protesters in Ottawa was significant, even if in reality there were only a few thousand. Therefore, it wasn't for tactical reasons that my highest priority was to get as many trucks onto Wellington as possible. It was to increase the perception of our support from average Canadians across the country. We would quickly learn it would have a global impact as well.

This also helped shape my next priority - morale. Having more Truckers right on Wellington, was absolutely great for morale. It gave us a sense of accomplishment to be standing on the footsteps of Parliament. When morale is high, you feel like you can accomplish almost anything and so do your fellow teammates. It's a natural high. There is no real downside to having high morale, especially if you are living in a truck during the middle of winter, for an unknown amount of time. I had a few occasions to address this with large groups on the street or in a conference room, so I borrowed a saying from the US Navy SEALs which is, "The only easy day was yesterday." As time went on, each day would become slightly more uncomfortable but we could overcome it by remembering why we were there in the first place. I also suggested that if they heard another Trucker complaining, gently tell them to stop feeling sorry for themself and ask them what will our discomfort be like two years from now if we give up today and don't go through this hardship now? When people start to feel sorry for their personal situation, that attitude spreads like an infection to others. We needed the Truckers to police themselves and to police each other's negative attitudes. We needed morale to remain high, but it wasn't always possible. I also wanted to appeal to the pride Truckers had for being rough and tough.

Obviously, if there was low morale, Truckers would start leaving and that would be bad for many reasons. One of the most important being, if we had fewer trucks on Wellington because people started disappearing in the middle of the night, it would leave gaps which would be visible on camera. At ground level, it's not as bad, but there was some incredible UAV footage going around on social media, and you couldn't hide missing trucks.

Media was my final priority. I knew there was a larger media plan being orchestrated somewhere, but in the early days, I didn't know what the specific plan was. I sensed that we needed to have two very clear strategies. One for social media and another for mainstream media (MSM). My feeling was that we would reward MSM, by giving them access, only if they gave good, honest coverage. We would punish them with no access if they lied. Having said that, dealing with MSM was not my responsibility, but when the time was right, I would express my views on it to the ones formulating a media plan. Also, I knew I had no ability to influence MSM, even if I wanted to.

I had watched a video about the Convoy, as it was traveling to Ottawa and the MSM was doing a story to try to make it look like the Convoy had little support. The reporter had his camera turned away from the large body of people on an overpass. One of the people on the overpass decided to take his own video and showed that the reporter was lying, by intentionally turning his camera away from the large crowd and only filming a small group of people standing off to the side. That personal video went viral. I knew MSM lied as easily as I inhaled a breath of air, so they couldn't be trusted.

There were some friendly media like Fox News in the US, who some of our team got great coverage from. Chris Barber appeared on Tucker Carlson. The coverage was accurate, and I was incredibly impressed with how good Chris was with the media.

Knowing we couldn't control MSM, I truthfully had no appetite to even engage with them, and lucky for me, my role didn't require it anyway. The one thing we could do was dominate social media. Prior to my arrival, I had only known about the Convoy from social media, and I knew it was our greatest strength in terms of communicating the truth, directly to our supporters around the country, and around the world.

During one of our first meetings, I was looking for feedback from Dana and Leanne to see what, if anything, the plan was for social media. From what I learned it was focusing on special events being planned to inform our supporters about what we were doing each day. This was where I first heard about TikTok. So naturally I downloaded the app and started monitoring certain people in the Convoy, like Chris Barber and others who each had enormous followings and were giving updates regularly.

It felt absolutely vital for us to share individual stories on video of as many Truckers as we could, through social media. We were getting letters of support from around the country, and I asked that the Truckers record those stories from their trucks and share them. Admittedly, I wanted to humanize the raw emotion of what Canadians were feeling through their support for the Truckers. I remember saying that I knew this was going to be emotional stuff for the Truckers reading the letters, but it was an important connection between them and supporting Canadians, who couldn't be in Ottawa.

About 10 days into my time at the Convoy I realized I had made a grave error with the order of my three priorities. "Morale" as my second priority was actually incorrect, but initially there was no clear way for me to have known. I had made assumptions regarding the ability of individual truck drivers to communicate with each other, as well as with us at the Arc Hotel. Admittedly, if I were to do it over again with a better understanding of the communication limitations, my second priority would have been "communications", not morale, because the number one contributor to low morale during the entire time of the Convoy, was our inability to communicate between what we were doing in the Arc Hotel and the individual Truckers on the streets.

There are three reasons why I made this critical error. One, Truckers carry CB radios. Two, everyone had cell phones and I kept hearing about them all using an app called Zello. It was my understanding at the time, that they were all communicating directly with each other on a large network. Additionally, people could simply speak to each other on the street and pass on information. As it turns out, messages from the Arc Hotel to the

Truckers were not getting passed at all.

As time went on, to our detriment, this problem was compounding daily but it would be days before we realized we had this monumental issue. Why? Because frustration was building on the streets and the Truckers didn't know who to talk to or who was in charge. They knew there were people somewhere planning something, but that was the extent of it. From their perspective, they were sitting in their trucks bored to tears day after day. Anyone who has been on guard duty knows that when you're sitting still and doing nothing, five minutes seems like an hour.

This was clearly a two-way communication problem. I didn't know they were not getting our messages, and I also didn't know they were struggling to pass their concerns on to us. How did this happen? They all had CBs, cell phones, and the ability to talk to each other on the streets. The biggest challenge was sending and receiving information from the Arc Hotel. We would only learn about this over time, when individual Truckers would come to the Arc Hotel, to express their deep frustrations, in person.

The lesson for me was that if I had ensured information was effectively being shared back and forth from the Arc Hotel to the Truckers, morale would have always remained incredibly high every day. This blind spot in my priorities, is directly attributed to confusion, frustration, and even anger from the Truckers, toward us in the Arc Hotel. All these things led to conflict and the incarnation of wildly imagined accusations with a touch of paranoia!

Chapter 5

Chaos, Egos and Icons

On day two of my arrival, I met Pat King. I had seen videos of his court cases several months before. I thought they were interesting but decided the information he shared wasn't as damaging to the Government as Pat had portrayed it. Regardless, I couldn't help being hopeful and I admired Pat's courage. Pat had given a lot of people hope, and with hope, courage soon follows. I liked Pat's energy and enthusiasm most of all.

It was already late in the afternoon, and I found myself with Pat and some others, planning to move more trucks onto

Wellington. Pat stated that he had a large group of trucks he was going to be leading into the city. It was difficult because the police had already started to erect concrete barricades all over the downtown core and mobility was getting tough. What we were looking at was filling up the streets perpendicular to Wellington first, then maybe getting some more trucks onto Wellington. The challenges we faced were plentiful. We had a lot of moving parts to this, and my concern was always safety for everyone, the police included.

One big challenge we had, was that many of the roads are one-way. So, going north to Wellington was more complex. Another issue was, the police had already blocked certain roads, so we had to account for that. The police also had the ability to easily relocate their cars and block any intersection once they detected our movements. It was obvious to me that we would have to do a slow roll through the city, sending multiple convoys to different intersections and then simultaneously turn north and go up as close to Wellington as possible. Another big concern was that we would have to do this at night and the road conditions were not great for big trucks. Safety again was always a big concern for me.

To develop this plan with Pat, I would have to give him a super crash course on War Gaming. In the Army, you have your G5 - Future Plans Officer, go against your G2 - Intelligence Officer. It is a simple process between your forces and the opponent's forces. Each team gets a turn to make a move or describe what they're going to do during a specified period of time. Sometimes the G2 who is playing your opponent gets the final turn, so you can plan for a final move or make a contingency to counter your opponent's final move. In this case, the opponent was the Ottawa Police who would be looking to stop us from getting more trucks into the downtown core.

It is very difficult to keep people from wanting to solve problems or pick apart an idea. The phrase "Yeah but," gets used a lot. In a War Gaming context, you want to say, "So what?" As in, "If this happens, so what?" Well, then you can take actions to counter that scenario. This is more of a deduction-based solution than picking apart an idea. It is a deliberate process and there must be at minimum, two people doing the War Game. You shouldn't do it alone, otherwise you would be playing as both players.

As Pat and I were working out the War Game on how to move these trucks, he paused and said, "Who are you, and how did you get here?" At first, I laughed and then I explained because the look on his face went from just talking, to all of a sudden, a look of suspicion. I explained who I was, and we just continued until he got a call and left the room.

I invested that time with Pat and in the end, the plan was never really executed. The trucks hadn't arrived with the expected numbers, and it seemed like planning for this was not nearly as fun to Pat, as just doing the move into the city and winging it as they went. It was a good reminder that I wasn't working with soldiers with years of training and discipline. I was dealing with some impulsive Truckers who just got things done and stayed away from "management types" whenever possible. That wasn't a criticism of Pat or anyone else. It was a sign that people were eager to make big moves as soon as possible.

We didn't have anyone guarding our conference room door, and it was a free-for-all in terms of access. This would soon be addressed because of an amazing man named Ray L. Ray took it upon himself to start guarding our conference room door, and his lovely wife Monique stayed by his side. He had seen the absolute chaos going in and out of the room and became frustrated by the fact that our meetings were always being highjacked by some sort of non-existent emergency. So, Ray used his own initiative to guard the door – and it had a huge impact on our ability to function more effectively. It was only after two weeks that I learned who Ray actually was, because we had a personal connection through mutual friends.

During the previous summer and fall, friends of mine had been attending these large potluck meetings with several like-minded people. They didn't like how the direction of the country was going and wanted to prepare for what may eventually come. These were not political meetings. They were about building mutually supportive communities, should the unvaccinated be completely excluded from society. These meetings are to this day, still happening at Ray's and all over Canada. Ray had been hosting them at his home for a long time and I was actually invited to the last two meetings to make connections and to see if I could contribute in a meaningful way. Regrettably, the timing didn't work out so I couldn't attend.

About two weeks into the Convoy, I was telling Ray about very close friends of mine, and he started asking me questions and we realized he knew them too. As soon as he told me they had attended his meetings, I knew exactly who he was. The beautiful thing about Ray is how humble he is. Once I knew who

Ray was in his community, I was embarrassed for how under utilized he had been for those last two weeks, but that is a testament to Ray's character. He had more than enough chances to take on a bigger role, but he saw an important need and took care of it without complaint. And there, is the true lesson. When you find someone who uses their initiative and doesn't need to be asked to do what's needed, don't ever let them go!

A few days later, I was in a meeting and asked Ray to keep everyone out of the room once it started. The meeting began and Ray secured the door. Pat King had just arrived and tried to get into the meeting. Ray told him no and Pat was really upset. He said to Ray, "I'm Pat King and I need to be in that meeting." To Ray's credit, he replied, "I don't care who you are. You're not getting in." From what Ray told me later, Pat returned with a much nicer demeanor and tried to charm his way into the meeting, but Ray stood his ground.

The thing about Pat's insistence on getting into that room was that he wasn't even invited to the meeting in the first place and would have likely been bored to tears. Had he arrived at the start, I would have allowed him in just to see if he had something to offer, because Pat has a leadership quality that people follow.

At the end of the Convoy, Pat was arrested and spent 150 days in jail, in Ottawa. He was charged with the same things as Tamara Lich - mischief, obstructing a peace officer, counseling others to commit mischief, counseling to commit intimidation, counseling to obstruct police, and blocking or obstructing one or more highways.

Chapter 6

My Replacement

On the night of February 2nd, Tamara came to the Arc where I had a conference room to work from. Her time was in demand, so I basically kicked everybody out of the room, locked the door, and we sat down with a coffee for our first real uninterrupted conversation. I could tell she was under a lot of stress over this big press conference everyone was pushing her to do the next day. At one point in the conversation she said, “People who know me think I'm a bit of a bitch, because I usually have my emotions under control. I don't cry.” But she had cried alone many times, and also in videos that went viral. What I didn't know at the time was that we would all cry at one point or another.

My advice to her was, "Blow the interview off. Don't do it tomorrow if you don't want to. Take some time off. Get away from everybody and clear your head. When you're ready, you'll do it. But not until you're ready for it."

I remember this conversation very distinctly because I couldn't identify with her feelings about her notoriety at the time. However, since the Convoy, I've thought about that conversation a lot. She told me, "Three weeks ago, I could walk down the street and nobody in the world had a clue who I was." With tears in her eyes, she expressed how "overwhelming and humbling" it was. She completely understood the enormous responsibility that was placed on her shoulders and said it was very difficult, because before the Freedom Convoy, nobody knew who she was, except for her friends and family. Now, she couldn't go down the street without people wanting to take a picture with her. It was celebrity status that she was not prepared for, and as I was sitting there thinking, "I have no concept of what that's about but thank God it's not me!"

I had no comprehension of what she was feeling. It wasn't even a consideration for me that I would ever enter a spotlight of any kind. I remember saying to someone, "When the history book is written about this Convoy, I'm perfectly okay if my name never appears in it."

Strangely, less than a week later I was doing live streams. My face was out there on the internet, and I was being slammed by the MSM for some poorly chosen words of mine. During that conversation with Tamara, I was trying to be supportive, and I had no personal experience with the magnitude of what she was feeling. The important thing is that I could tell she felt the massive responsibility to our supporters weighing heavily on her.

---

3 February 2022

Tamara agreed to do the big press conference at the Marriott Hotel the next day. She was hesitant to do it, but she did it anyway. Jack McClellan, who I knew from my time with Police on Guard, and I, wanted to go watch it live. We knew it was going to be a very big deal because the MSM was invited, and they actually attended.

As we arrived, we just kind of followed the gaggle. Although there was a room for the actual press conference, as I walked in with Jack everyone was out in the hallway getting organized.

The room was full. Rebel News was there, but I didn't know who the majority of the other people were, why they were there, or what they had to do with any of this press conference.

There was also this group of five suits. I had no idea who these people were at the time but they turned out to be lawyers employed by JCCF, and Keith Wilson, who was under contract to them. As I studied everyone in the room who was interacting with Tamara, Danny Bulford, and Joanie, a French-speaking truck captain from Quebec, I figured out who amongst the lawyers, was the person in charge. I didn't know then who Keith Wilson was, I just knew he was directing everyone in terms of this press conference. He and Eva Chipiuk were the two who really stood out. As I watched Keith orchestrating the speaking order and how everyone was going to walk in, I looked over to Jack and said, “You see all those lawyers over there? They’re my replacement. I'll be going home in a day or two.”

Jack and I went into the press conference room and as I watched the setup, I saw all the media surrounding the podium. Keith did the introductions and turned the microphone over to Tamara. As Tamara started talking, my stomach was in knots. I couldn’t believe how cool she was under pressure. I don’t impress easily, but Tamara impressed the hell out of me with her calmness. I was glad it wasn’t me up there at that podium. As Tamara was giving that statement like an absolute professional, I remember thinking I would be terrified to do what she was doing. Later I asked her how she remained so composed, and she simply answered, “God”. She told me she felt such a calming sense of purpose and wasn’t nervous at all. I was nervous enough for both of us!

Joanie, the road captain from Quebec, read the same statement in French to ensure we were not forgetting our French-speaking supporters. Then Danny took over and gave a brief introduction about himself and an update on the Convoy regarding public safety. I later found out that Keith had asked Danny to do this to reduce the number of people speaking and to ease tensions by conveying a sense of careful consideration for public safety and professionalism from the organizers.

The statements concluded and then Keith opened it up for questions from the floor. Right from the start, an obnoxious member of the MSM, started shouting absolutely ridiculous questions at Tamara. Jim Torma, who was working for the PPC at the time, got into a shouting match with the media person and the room erupted into chaos. Keith immediately ended the press conference and escorted Tamara, Joanie, and Danny out of the room.

Jack and I ended up back at the Arc Hotel and I headed into the conference room on the main floor. We'd been working in that conference room for quite some time, and now the lawyers were there and had taken over our space. I had no idea who told them to go there, but I was honestly relieved to see they would be co-located with me, instead of being at The Swiss Hotel. While I was glad they were there, they came in like a tornado and really made people uncomfortable. They had a real sense of urgency and purpose and didn't have time to make people feel warm and fuzzy. As far as I was concerned, I was prepared to step aside if I believed someone more capable than me was taking over. I wasn't in Ottawa for ego, I was there for my children, and I wanted the very best people up front, and if that wasn't me, so be it.

On the morning of February 2nd, part of the legal team had flown on a private charter from Edmonton, Alberta, with stops in Medicine Hat to get Tamara's husband Dwayne, Saskatoon to pick up two lawyers, Regina to get an Accountant who Tamara had already enlisted to help, Winnipeg for another lawyer, and Thunder Bay to refuel. The plane arrived in Ottawa at approximately 10 p.m. EST.

The accountant had already been handling the details of the crowdfunding campaign before this trip, and while on the plane to Ottawa, informed the others that the GoFundMe campaign had been suspended by the crowdfunding giant! GoFundMe's concern was that the money was being used to fund illegal activities, even though it was well known that they had worked with BLM without issue.

When the five-lawyer team arrived at the Arc Hotel, they were given a further brief of the situation in Ottawa, at about 11:30 p.m. This was when the lawyers learned about the press conference Tamara was expected to give the next day. That press conference had been organized by a very diverse group of people from all walks of life called, Taking Back Our Freedoms (TBOF). TBOF was co-founded in Alberta by a solid guy named Roy Beyer, who had amassed several highly credentialed medical experts, and well-known politicians, including the former Premier of Newfoundland, Brian Peckford.

Laura Baden Ph.D. was also with TBOF. Laura is as feisty as she is brilliant. She is a molecular biologist with a focus on immunology. Her husband Patrick was with her in Ottawa and the two of them made an incredible team. We spent several hours together planning future public statements I would have to make.

Under the original plan, Tamara would make a joint statement with Paul Alexander Ph.D., and Dr. Rodger Hodkinson, M.D. The legal team, looking at it from the lens of their clients only, wanted to reduce the message down to a much more succinct statement and felt that adding the medical aspect of the press conference would complicate the overall first public statement given by the Convoy leaders.

To say this caused some confusion and hard feelings would be an understatement. Unfortunately, this could have all been mitigated had the lawyers been in Ottawa sooner and been given more time to acclimate themselves. Unfortunately, this was just not possible.

I sat down and started to study the map of the city and contemplate what was happening in the streets. Keith later recounted his first memory of me. He looked around the room, which was just going crazy, and thought, "There's this guy, sitting there in the middle of the chaos, looking at the map, totally focused and concentrating. I don't know who that guy is, but I'm going to keep an eye on him."

My first impression of Eva reminded me of Murphy Brown. Very professional, probably a corporate killer, with a sense of humor. At one point I got up to get a coffee from a table on the opposite wall to where I was seated. Eva came toward me, fully consumed by her iPhone. She had no idea who I was, and likely wouldn't have cared, but I said to her, "When you get a moment, I need to speak to you about some issues." She looked up just enough to politely acknowledge me. I waited until she finally came around to my side of the table and asked again, "Do you have some time for me?" And of course, she had her cell phone in her hand, she said, "Yeah", and kept texting. So, I just looked at her and said, "I'll wait." She sent the text, and I started talking again and then she brought the phone back up to text again. Very patiently I said, "I don't get the impression that I have your attention right now." And she hesitated and said, "Let me just finish this and I'll stop." I couldn't help but immediately like her in that moment, even though I had to risk being rude to get her attention.

Keith noticed that her body language completely changed and he realized, “I know she's listening to that guy. That guy’s a player in this because Eva would never have stopped if he wasn’t telling her something important.” When we finished our conversation, Eva immediately walked over to Keith saying, “You need to talk to that guy.” Right there and then, we became ‘The Three Amigos’ for the remainder of our time in Ottawa, even if we didn’t know it at the time.

Keith and Eva stuck around for the entire time the Convoy was in Ottawa. Shortly after they arrived, the other three lawyers went back home, potentially because they didn't want to get caught in this future legal nightmare. I couldn’t blame them.

Because of my time in the army, I knew that lawyers always have a seat at the table. You have to have lawyers at your table when you're at war, to make sure you don't violate the Laws of Armed Conflict. While we were not at war, I intuitively knew we needed them in the decision-making loop as the situation was obviously evolving.

In a military context during war, if you're deliberately going to attack somebody - a high-priority target or person - a commander and his staff will conduct something called the Targeting Board. Lawyers have to be involved to make sure you don't commit a crime against humanity or destroy culturally significant infrastructure. You have to have your legal team advising you on what the repercussions of your actions could be. Legal advice is not the only factor, but its incredibly important in terms of accountability.

Logically, I thought if I had lawyers available to me, I was going to use them for every major decision I might need to make, and if I was making recommendations to others. For example, I had already been working on a plan with Randy Hillier, to park tractors on the front lawn of the Supreme Court the very next day.

A few nights before, I had done a walk on Wellington with Dana Metcalf and Leanne Carter. I needed to get out of the Arc Hotel and clear my head while checking on the physical layout of our trucks on Wellington and the surrounding area. It was becoming a real challenge for me to do this because of everything happening inside the Arc Hotel which was preventing me from getting out during the day. I took the two others with me in case I was arrested as I wanted someone to know I had been taken. I got a great update from them on what they were experiencing on the streets every day too. Shortly after getting to Wellington, the three of us got separated.

I stopped walking right in front of the east entrance gate on Parliament Hill and started to read some of the hundreds of stories people had put along the wall. The stories were incredibly gut-wrenching because they were personal stories of despair and tragedy. As I stood there reading all of these stories, I looked past the wall at the Parliament building in the background and it gave me such a sickening feeling throughout my entire body, as if the realization that something evil had overtaken the intended purpose of what that building once represented to me as a Canadian.

In a surreal moment of sadness, I turned to look behind me at a young French-Canadian man shoveling the sidewalk around his truck. I hadn't noticed how emotional I had become when Leanne found me and asked me if I was okay. Lucky for me, the truck I was standing near had just started and the diesel exhaust got into my eyes, which gave me an instant cover story for rubbing the tears away from my face.

We walked west on Wellington because it was starting to get late. As I looked at the ground in front of the Supreme Court, I realized I could park a whole bunch of stuff on the front lawn and get right up to the front steps. It was a terrifying and bold idea, which would require a lot of consideration, most of all to determine if the risk, versus reward was worth it in the long run.

I was thinking, who could I get to do this? Who could, or who would, be willing to take on this task, are two different considerations. So, my first thought was Pat King would do it! But who else? I knew that Randy Hillier was having an event where he was inviting a bunch of farmers to bring their tractors to Ottawa, and he had already made the announcement for a big rally and invited all the farmers with their tractors.

I looked at both and thought, if I ask Pat King to do it, he's going to park a bunch of trucks right on the front lawn. He'll do it because he's crazy enough to do it, but what worried me was that Pat would get hurt because the Parliamentary Protective Police were right around the corner. Security was literally on the other side of the building, and they would have been there and responded to him immediately. I was very worried for his personal safety, and I was afraid that he could possibly get killed by the police or that somebody else could get hurt. So, I decided I wasn't going to ask Pat King.

Randy, however, is an elected official. I also considered the fact that the ground at that time of year, usually could have taken transport trucks, but on the day I wanted to do this, it was warmer, and I was a bit concerned that trucks would have a hard time getting onto the lawn and possibly get bogged down. So I thought, Randy was bringing tractors that are custom-made for this kind of ground. It won't be a problem at all. Randy was an elected MPP, and he'd already called all the tractors to be there on Saturday. He had the right vehicles to go onto that ground if it did turn soft. Lastly, I knew the tractors would only be a very temporary stay on the lawn, as they were only there for the day to support us and Randy. I decided it had to be Randy and his tractors. But I also had to let people know because it wasn't only my decision to make. My ultimate goal was to consolidate vehicles onto Wellington, in order to put maximum pressure on the Federal Government. Ideally, we would have been able to use the tractors to negotiate with the OPS to allow us to get the port-a-potties emptied, which they were preventing from happening.

I started working on the plan with Randy and he said, "Yep, let's do it!" without hesitation. After some planning and coordination with Randy, I was within an hour of telling him to execute the plan, but I said, "Before I green light this, I've got to check with the lawyers." So I went to Eva, and of course she was texting. I said, "I need to tell you something. You're the last person in my checkbox to confirm this with. I want you to know that within the hour I'm going to green light a plan to park a bunch of tractors on the front lawn of the Supreme Court. You have five minutes to convince me why I shouldn't do this." She looked up at me and says bluntly, "No, you're not." And it took her only thirty seconds to convince me why not.

Very early in the Convoy, there was a matter before a judge to get an injunction to stop the Truckers from honking horns. Eva had already faced Justice McLean in his court room over the horn injunction, and she was firm in her opinion about what I wanted to do.

I can't quote her exact words, but they were something like, "You're not going to park a bunch of anything on the front lawn of the Supreme Court - desecrate the Holy Grail of law, their sacred ground - and then think I'm going in front of Justice McLean over this horn injunction and not be punished. You think you're not going to prejudice my case? The judge is going to lose his mind if you do this. You're going to piss off a judge by parking things right up to the front steps of the most significant symbol of law in this country, and you think that the judge isn't going to take it out on me? Every time I stepped into a courtroom from now on, we'd get punished by the judges for doing it. You'll never get them to support you again. They're going to just look at you like a terrorist."

She was absolutely correct, and the smartest thing I could have done was get her input.

To say that I got verbally slapped is an understatement! I called it off because I knew she was in a tough spot with McLean, and in the end, we would just have to find a more palatable way to pressure the government.

In September 2022, Keith and Eva were in Ottawa for the "Mootness" hearing for Brian Peckford's lawsuit against the Federal Government's violation of his Charter of Rights and Freedoms, Section 6, Mobility Rights. I went to Ottawa to see them because they were so close. On the second night we were there, I walked with Eva down Wellington to the Supreme Court building, and I showed her and said, "Look at it. You can get everything through here. I could have gone over that curb, right in between all these concrete barriers. It would have been nothing. I could've gotten right up front. I might have even been able to crawl up the steps!" In fairness to Eva, she did remind me that they would have probably invoked The Emergencies Act much sooner if we had taken that approach.

In hindsight, especially after hearing some of the testimony during the POEC, I wonder if I should have done it anyway.

Chapter 7

Rhetoric and No Tangible Results

I woke up early on the morning of February 5th to several messages with a link to the Ottawa Police Services Board Meeting from the previous night. What I heard from the President of the Board, Diane Deans, was absolutely horrifying. She used some incredibly inflammatory rhetoric, to say the least. But what I was most interested in was the Chief of Police, Peter Sloly's response.

In Ontario, a Police Services Board typically hires a Police Chief who is technically their boss, with one exception. A Board member, comprised of elected city councilors, is forbidden from directing police operations in terms of criminal investigations. We cannot have a situation where politicians are directing the police to investigate people they don't like, especially political opponents and protesters. This measure is put in place to protect the police when they're conducting investigations. They must remain impartial to the whims of unethical politicians. It also allows the police to investigate any potential criminal activity of a sitting politician.

Deans opened up with some wildly outrageous comments from a prepared statement she read to the audience.

"We're on Day 8 of this occupation. Our city is under siege. This group is emboldened by the lack of enforcement by every level of government. They are terrorizing our residents. Torturing them with incessant honking, threatening them, and preventing them from leading their lives. People cannot go to work or open their businesses. They cannot sleep, walk, shop, go to medical appointments, or enjoy their neighborhood. This group is a threat to our democracy. What we're seeing is bigger than just a city of Ottawa problem. This is a nationwide insurrection. This is madness. We need a concrete plan to put an end to this."

As Sloly reflected back on her words, he provided a summary of what he had heard. I believed he was doing that for the record to show his understanding of her motivation.

"A city under siege. This is a threat to our democracy. It's a nationwide insurrection. This is madness."

Chief Sloly continued to walk a fine line throughout the rest of the meeting, to attempt to appease his boss. It was absolutely unclear to me at that time, how he was going to respond in a practical sense and how that was going to impact us.

During Chief Sloly's testimony at the POEC, we learned that as early as February 2, 2022, he had informed the political apparatus in the city that the Freedom Convoy, "the solution may not be a policing one".

From my very limited perspective, one thing that was abundantly clear to me, after watching Diane Deans in this meeting, was that we needed to do everything in our power to take some pressure off Chief Sloly. It was obvious that the pressure on him was mounting. If his position changed, because of the pressure he was under from the Board, it would get much worse for everyone involved.

I wasn't the only one who noticed. Randy Hillier called me too and advised it was time to start talking to the city to see if we could get some progress, because the Federal Liberal leadership was nowhere to be seen.

Initially, I had zero interest in talking to the local politicians and thought it might be a waste of time. I didn't see them as having any authority to remove Covid restrictions, but they did have access to the right people, and the PMO.

I spoke to Keith and Eva about what I observed from this meeting. After watching the first ten minutes of the Police Services Board meeting, Keith also made the same observation, that the pressure on Sloly was getting ridiculous. We didn't know how, but we intuitively understood that we needed to reduce the pressure on Sloly.

Keith had spoken to Brian Peckford, the former Premier of Newfoundland. Peckford is the last living signature of the Charter of Rights and Freedoms, written in 1982. Premier Peckford also made the same recommendation to us that Randy did, about talking to the city. Keith asked Premier Peckford if he had any contacts that we could use to start doing some back channeling between us and the city. Had Randy, Keith, and Premier Peckford not all made the same recommendation at the same time, I likely wouldn't have bothered with the city and just continued to work with the OPS.

As it turned out, Premier Peckford put Keith in contact with Dean French, former Chief-of-Staff to Doug Ford, the current Premier of Ontario. In negotiations or any form of diplomacy, you have to start small and find out if there is even any appetite to negotiate. In this case, we couldn't just walk to the mayor's office and expect a welcome from him. We had to find an intermediary who would speak for both of us to see if there was any opportunity to engage in a meaningful dialogue.

As it turns out, there would be. We just had to be very careful because we all knew we couldn't trust the Mayor of Ottawa, Jim Watson, because of the public statements he had already made about the Convoy. He had written a letter to Trudeau and Mendicino, on the 7th, stating "The demonstration has turned into an aggressive and hateful occupation of our neighborhoods." It was for actions like this that I had no interest in dealing with him directly. I was mostly interested in dealing with the unelected officials.

More symbolically than anything, on February 6, 2022, the City of Ottawa declared a State of Emergency. In actuality, this didn't give the City any special authority other than to convey to the residents that the mayor was taking the situation seriously.

Part of acting responsibly, was for the Convoy to also recognize the human factors in policing. We were very cognizant that despite being on opposite sides for the moment, we were also fighting for the very rights of each police officer, while the police themselves were possibly going to take the rights away from us all. Nevertheless, we had to do whatever we could to take the pressure off Chief Sloly, so his officers would not escalate their interactions with us in non-productive ways.

Unfortunately, the OPS decided to make a move that I believe was absolutely foolish and counter-productive. Just two nights later, on February 6, 2022, they sent their entire Public Order Unit or POU with Snipers and UAVs to raid one of our staging areas at Coventry.

Coventry was the parking lot for the city's large baseball park. On the first day of the Convoy, many trucks were diverted there and it turned into an outstanding camp with hundreds of people and even more supplies. We had three other locations as well, fully stocked with thousands of pounds of supplies for an indefinite stay. We referred to them as "88" which is east of Ottawa near Embrum, "Arnprior" and the "Parkway". We were not centrally located and 88 and Arnprior were both private properties. In the early days of the Convoy, there were too many people to count in Arnprior, but when the police were clearing the city at the end, there were approximately 200 people and about seventy vehicles. One Friday night in Arnprior, there was a church service and a concert held with about 500 people in attendance. At eighty-eight on average there was typically 100 vehicles and about 200 people.

Coventry was closest to the downtown area, and it was easiest to distribute supplies from there. During the testimony at the POEC, I was incredibly frustrated to hear how the city officials described Coventry and also made some very grotesque statements about how we had dangerously stored all the fuel there. This was a ridiculous statement, given the Fire Department had inspected how we were storing the fuel there on the 5th and 7th of February. Additionally, the Electrical Safety Authority, ESA, had also completed an inspection of our generator and large electrical panel, at a cost of almost $300. We passed both the Fire Inspection and the ESA inspections at Coventry. Again, this is what acting responsibly meant to the leadership at Coventry.

I woke up on the 6th after having very little sleep. The night before, I had been in a very long meeting, for which the subject of the meeting is now a blur. Unfortunately, it was decided that this meeting would be confidential, and therefore no cell phones were allowed. I had assumed all our phones were being tapped and really had nothing to hide. In some cases, people felt uncomfortable talking around a cell phone, so we often left them in the hallway on a table. I remember joking with one of the OPS Officers that they were probably listening in on our calls and he jokingly said they were. After the awkward laugh, it confirmed to me that they were listening in. If I was in their position, I would have been listening too, and I filed that away in my mind. Luckily, I never had to. If I wanted to build some trust with them, I didn't want to engage in deception.

I'm normally attached to my cellphone, because of my son's health. Over the years, I've spent more nights in the ER with him, than I can possibly remember. Against my comfort, I did leave my phone outside of the meeting room, because the group of people in the meeting requested it.

Foolishly, I didn't have a plan in place for being away from my phone in case something happened with my kids. That's exactly when I needed it. My son's mother was trying to reach me because she had called an ambulance to take him to the hospital. She couldn't reach me, so she called my daughter's mother to get hold of me. Unfortunately, that didn't work either. Thankfully, my son was back home at 5 a.m. on the morning of the 6th. As much as I regret my son going to the ER, that experience further reinforced my strong determination to keep as many safety lanes open on the streets of Ottawa, as possible. It was personal for me, and I was absolutely determined to ensure that no one would ever be denied access to emergency services of any kind.

I was relieved to hear the testimony of Ottawa officials during the POEC, not the politicians but actual first responders, confirming they did not have any issues with getting to emergency situations. Just prior to the Convoy, Inspector Russell Lucas from the OPS had moved into the Operations Support Inspector role, which oversees the Special Events Section as well as other operations support units such as Tactical, K9, and Emergency Services. He testified that by the first weekend, they were able to keep intersections and safety lanes open and buses operating and this didn't change until after The Emergencies Act was invoked.

Leanne Carter had a good friend named Anna, who was looking for a way to help out with the Convoy and she just happened to live in Ottawa. From that day forward, Anna went everywhere I went. I then explained to my daughter's mother that it was possible a woman would be answering my phone when I wasn't available, as I didn't want her thinking the worst while I was away from home. It was understood that it was just a contingency plan that needed to be in place because of what had happened with my son.

During the evening of the 6th, I was on a Zoom call with many people, when I was notified that the OPS was currently raiding Coventry. I informed everyone what I had just learned, left the call, then Jack McClellan and I immediately headed to Coventry in his car. The OPS had an outer cordon set up and wouldn't allow vehicles into the area when we tried to drive there, but we were allowed to walk in. I walked a few hundred meters to Coventry and Jack stayed with his car until we reconnected later. Laura-Lynn Tyler Thompson, Podcast host and Freedom Activist, was also on that Zoom call and had arrived at Coventry before us. She was already live-streaming the raid when I arrived.

I have to say, I was absolutely baffled as to why the OPS had made a stupid move like that. They achieved nothing, other than to help us gain even more support from Canadians.

The police arrived in a large bus with full tactical gear and assault rifles. We could see snipers on the hotel roof adjacent to the baseball park, as well as UAVs hovering over top. To my knowledge there were no arrests, but the police did steal several hundred liters of fuel and for some reason, they took some of the food supplies.

It wasn't until after the police started their retreat from the area that I learned, they had stolen regular fuel for the generators, not the fuel we were using in the trucks. This entire operation achieved nothing in terms of stopping our ability to keep going. Our sustainment plan was still firmly in place!

Before leaving, I spoke to a few of the leaders who were running Coventry and asked that they consider moving a few trucks to block the entrances of the parking lot once the police left. We knew it wouldn't stop them from getting in again, but it would at least make it more difficult for them next time. Of note, there was absolutely no appetite for giving the police a reason to make arrests. For the most part, the crowd was satisfied with just yelling their discontent with the police and their actions. What I found very telling, was that the police officers would not make eye contact with any of us. While I fundamentally disagree with their actions, at least they conducted themselves professionally while executing the raid. Professional or not, their entire operation was completely counterproductive and likely just an attempt to be seen as doing something, even if that something accomplished nothing of value.

It was that evening, that I broke my own rule of speaking

publicly during my time at the Convoy. Laura-Lynn saw me getting into Jack's car and asked for a comment while she was live streaming the raid. That was the very first time I ever appeared on a live stream in my entire life. When Jack and I returned to the Arc Hotel, I briefed the team on the situation and further reinforced that we were completely fine. I have no idea who decided we needed to do a live stream of our own, to reassure the public that we were still able to keep going. It was suggested that I speak to our supporters and explain our position and what was happening.

I initially declined, and many people immediately volunteered to do it in my place. While I personally didn't care about who spoke, I was very concerned about what that message might be. Given the OPS would have been watching, I wanted to make sure our response was very calm and well-considered. This was an opportunity to let them know their efforts were wasted and did more to harm their position, than ours. So, upon further consideration, I decided I would speak briefly about what had just transpired at Coventry. It was decided that several others would also speak. I didn't have an issue with this plan, I just wanted to make sure the message about our ability to continue was abundantly clear to our supporters.

It was decided that Dr. Roger Hodkinson, Dr. Paul Alexander, and Jeff Bouvine would go ahead of me, and I would end the livestream with a brief closing remark. Surprisingly, Joseph Bourgault also spoke during that live stream, and I was very impressed by what he said and how well he said it. I hadn't spent enough time with him, but I knew he was someone I would work with more closely when given the chance.

The live stream had gone off without any issues and it was well attended. What I didn't realize was that my participation in that live stream, was unintentionally, my audition for the camera. The very next day, I made a detailed and prepared statement to the public on my first formal live stream, which was also broadcast, by Lincoln Jay from Rebel News and a few others in the room.

Shortly after the Coventry raid, we were informed that bringing fuel into the city for our trucks would not be permitted. Well, Canadians are industrious and this situation proved it! This marked the arrival of a new and immediately popular fashion accessory – the "jerry can"!

Thousands of supporters started carrying jerry cans from home into the city. Some were filled with fuel, others with water, and some with a variety of creative drinks. I had even seen a few that were used to collect cash our supporters were bringing in on weekends. I remember seeing a rather intoxicated guy drinking out of a jerry can funnel, and he was certainly happy to be there.

Our team from the Arc Hotel, Jeff Bouvine, and Leanne Carter, went to the local Canadian Tire stores and bought hundreds of jerry cans to flood the city. It seemed to work perfectly in terms of countering the police, who from what I understand, thought it was equally amusing and didn't do too much to bother the people carrying a jerry can. Word got out that the Police would start confiscating jerry cans, but I didn't hear many reports of it happening, other than two of our members were arrested for "aiding and abetting" because they were carrying fuel cans. Still, we were very careful not to flaunt it when we were giving fuel to the Truckers.

On the morning of February 7th, I had my regularly scheduled 10 a.m. phone call with Constable Andrew Wierzbicki from the OPP. In that conversation, I expressed my sincere disappointment in the OPS for executing such a counterproductive plan, in terms of building mutual trust between us and them. I had to be very careful with my words because I did not want them to be perceived as a threat in any way. The message I needed to convey was that we didn't want to engage in a tit-for-tat scenario.

As respectfully as I could, I told him, "We will never exceed the level of stupidity that you guys are directing at us. We might match it, but we'll never exceed it. And by the way, your Coventry raid was your freebie. We're not going to do anything because of what you did at Coventry, as we don't see the value in it. We don't want to escalate this into something terrible."

However, just to prove the point, we did conduct slow rolls of small convoys to a few locations. It wasn't meant to be antagonistic. It was to demonstrate that we could impact them too. One of the places we went to, was the Ottawa Airport. We knew that many of the Federal MPs traveled home on Friday evenings so we felt it was just enough to make them at least consider that they might not be able to get home. But to be clear, we had already decided we would never have shut down the airport because it was deemed critical infrastructure and the blowback would have been counterproductive and severe.

Pat King was the leader of that slow roll, but he was accompanied by Tom Quiggin to make sure that nothing went wrong. Tom is also a retired soldier and former intelligence analyst for the federal government. He's brilliant and highly dependable so I asked him to go to make sure things stayed under control.

I was advised that there was only one way in and out for the air ambulance and I wanted to have guarantees that we would not go anywhere near that area of the airport. I didn't think Pat would do anything to disrupt the air ambulance, but I asked Tom to go because we needed a high level of assurance that nothing would be antagonistic, causing the OPS to respond unfavorably. We also did a slow roll through the Amazon distribution center in Ottawa. Our thinking was that the MPs might get a few phone calls from the Amazon executives and make the MPs feel the pressure from that angle as well. If they weren't going to talk to us, we found some pressure points to apply.

Again, the goal wasn't to be overtly hostile and threatening. Instead, it was to say that we had moves too, and we would only do things if they continued to do stupid things like raid our compounds and steal our supplies. I told them we wouldn't do tit-for-tat, but they needed to understand that we could do that too.

Chapter 8

First Public Statement

To this day, I can't remember who told me I was doing a live stream, on Monday the 7th, but I very reluctantly agreed to do it. As a military officer and a recently fired teacher, it was very common for me to speak to groups of people and it was easy for me in most settings. For some reason, this was very different from any other public speaking situation I had ever been involved in.

I had spent the day in various meetings, but the hot topic was that Keith and Eva would appear before Justice McLean over the horn injunction. Ultimately Justice McLean ruled that people stop honking the horns.

For some unknown reason, I did not get the message about the horn injunction until at least another day.

However, in his ruling, he also wrote "This Court Orders that, provided the terms of the Order are complied with, the Defendants and other persons remain at liberty to engage in a peaceful, lawful, and safe protest."

To many of us, this was a huge victory. To some, it was a little frustrating because they wanted to continue with the horns, as a means of putting pressure on the Government. I didn't see it that way, because we just had a Judge rule, we had a right to be there, as long as we abided by the horn injunction. Some Truckers initially refused to comply with the Order, but eventually, people got the message.

There was one particular truck driver, right beside the stage on Wellington, who would not comply. It wasn't until Chris Barber and a few other Truckers showed up with tools and told the guy if he didn't stop, they would remove the horn from his truck. In truth, most of us, especially Chris, were getting very tired of the horns so this gave us a graceful way out of honking the horns anyway!

In the late afternoon of the 7th, I was able to find some time to go to my hotel room with Dr. Laura Braden and her husband Patrick. Laura and Patrick were there from P.E.I and were an absolute Godsend couple to work with. Laura had been part of TBOF and was there with many of the other doctors and scientists.

We spent about an hour writing the statement I would make on the live stream. I was accompanied by Chris Barber, with Lincoln Jay from Rebel News being the only known news agency to cover it. We had our own people live streaming it from their phones as well because they had large social media audiences.

PUBLIC STATEMENT

"Good morning. My name is Tom Marazzo. I've been asked to make a statement on behalf of Freedom Convoy 2022.

On Saturday, the Police Services Board for the City of Ottawa met with the City Chief of Police, to plan a way forward to end the peaceful demonstration in their city. I would like to review some of the language that was used by members during the meeting. Specifically, Diane Deans, the chair of the Police Services Board. She mischaracterized Ottawa as, and I quote, "A city under siege, with its democracy threatened, during a nationwide insurrection, that was driven by madness."

These alarmist words were directed at Canadians who are here peacefully protesting and just want their freedoms restored. This is not a time for hysterics by municipal politicians. All the polling that we have seen affirms to us that Canadians want us here. Over 100 downtown residents have come forward with signed legal affidavits. They have described accurately the peaceful nature of this freedom protest.

As a volunteer of this movement to restore our freedoms, I have been coordinating with Ottawa police, the Ontario

Provincial Police, the RCMP, and the Parliament Hill Protective Services, to help Canadians who have come to Ottawa from coast to coast, to ensure this protest is both responsible and safe.

At approximately 6:30 p.m. last night, an estimated 100 officers in full tactical gear, snipers mounted on adjoining roofs, and UAV drones flying overhead, aggressively raided one of our minor supply depots. They proceeded to confiscate donated and purchased fuel that was destined for our supporters. This action was a direct result of the Police Services Board's interference with Police operations.

This was not responsible. This was not safe.

It was an unnecessary, misguided, aggressive show of force meant to intimidate Canadians who were exerting their Charter Rights and Freedoms in their nation's capital.

The rhetoric that was publicly displayed during the Police Services Board meeting on Saturday was not representative of the great lengths that we worked to achieve over the last nine days with the Ottawa Police.

On Saturday in the city of Winnipeg, an angry citizen, reported by the media as a member of Antifa, drove a vehicle into a crowd of demonstrators, striking down four people. This was tragic, foreseeable, and quite possibly could have been prevented. We cannot set the conditions for that to happen in Ottawa.

We have consistently communicated to all Police departments since the beginning that this protest can only be resolved through political dialogue, not police action. What all Canadians want is not within the power of the Chief of Ottawa police to give. This can only be resolved by lawmakers, not tyrannical enforcement. After ten days of peaceful protesting, it is time to sit at a table and plan a way forward. We are calling for a delegation from the City of Ottawa to meet with us this Tuesday, February 8th. As a sign of good faith, we are willing to reduce the honking of horns to five minutes per day, commencing at 5:00 p.m.. If the residents of Ottawa are hearing horns at 12:01 p.m. on Tuesday, tomorrow, you will know that their two governments have no interest in resolving this.

Every time the police conduct an aggressive operation against us, the support for this movement only grows. As was seen in Toronto and other cities across Canada this past weekend.

The responsible course of action now is for the city of Ottawa to sit at a table and start a meaningful dialogue and to de-escalate aggressive police action and work with us to resolve this responsibly. Thank you."

I have to admit, for some inexplicable reason, I was absolutely terrified. Before we began, I didn't ask if it was live or recorded. After I started speaking, I noticed a live smartphone off to the side. That was the moment when I thought I was about to vomit all over the desk in front of me. To this day, I can't understand why I felt that way. I just know I was terrified throughout that live stream, as well as the rest of the public statements I'd do while in Ottawa. During another live stream, I couldn't pronounce a specific word after repeatedly trying and finally had to just choose a different word altogether. It was a rather odd Porky-Pig moment for me. Thankfully I had prepared, and all I had to do was read from the paper if I got myself into trouble while speaking.

During that live stream with Chris, many of my prepared statements were directed at the police themselves. This is a typical tactic used in negotiations. You use whatever media is available to signal your intentions directly or indirectly to those you are negotiating with, and this was the perfect opportunity to do that, especially after the Coventry raid.

Additionally, the public had not seen me before and I knew this would have an impact on gaining further support. The same is true for the police services that would have been watching too. While I was dealing daily with the OPS and OPP Liaison Officers, this would give the rest of their leadership a chance to see and measure the types of people coming and helping the original Freedom Convoy organizers. I don't say this out of ego. Quite the contrary. I was anticipating a psychological impact on their thinking. I say this because until then, the police leadership was accustomed to thinking they were dealing with "blue-collar workers", not military officers trained in tactics and operational planning. To be honest, I can't say that it made a difference to them at all, or that an army officer changed anything, but if it was me on the other side, it would have had an impact on my approach to planning.

From my perspective, Tamara is the coolest person I've ever seen under that kind of pressure, and she easily delivered her words like they were gospel. Chris Barber had been outstanding and very articulate on Fox News, as well as on his TikTok channel. The difference between my effort and theirs was hopefully, that the psychological impact of my former profession as an army officer, might change the dynamics with the police – not Tom Marazzo the individual. I felt that fact would create an effect on them in a few different ways. Again, "Tom" would not have an impact on them, but an army officer might. Whether that is true or not, it was what I was going for.

I wanted to let them all know that the Convoy was being supported by some serious players who were not afraid to push back against the police and government for what they had done to this country. I was also expecting the police leadership would feel the same way about Danny Bulford and Tom Quiggin. As time when on, and our military veterans started to show up in Ottawa, I was hoping it was going to have an impact on the rank-and-file police officers on the street, especially when they saw the veterans showing up with their berets and medals.

First, they would quickly know that we were trained in this type of operational planning and knew we could disrupt their plans as easily as they could disrupt ours. Secondly, I wanted them to realize that we were an experienced team they could work with to make this safe for all. We were not reckless; we were responsible, and focused on the real issues that were the reason for being there. They just had to take us seriously and we could all get what we wanted, safely and responsibly.

In terms of the first live stream I did, I knew my demeanor was very different than what the public had seen so far. I looked and spoke differently than the other notable people in the Convoy. I'm not a truck driver, I'm a retired military officer and teacher, with public speaking training and experience. I presented an image of what anyone from my background would expect to see. I'm not better, I'm simply different.

After the Convoy ended, I was told that the overall perception of the Convoy had changed when I started doing the live streams. Beforehand, people were not sure if we were truly the "fringe minority" we'd been dubbed by the Prime Minister. Controversial people like Pat King were in the forefront doing a lot of social media that people were tuning in to hear.

Things changed when people like me, Danny Bulford, Tom Quiggin, and Eddy Cornel started speaking publicly. Again, not better, just different. In truth, I don't think we could have gained the support we did if we didn't each show ourselves to be from such a wide range of different backgrounds in our society. We were doctors, lawyers, retired police, and military, as well as every other white and blue-collar worker you could imagine.

In the early days of the Convoy, before my public statements, I always felt like my two OPS Liaison Officers treated me like a low-level dime bagger, at 2 a.m. on some street corner. I didn't feel like I was being taken very seriously. In one of my meetings with them, they started arguing with each other in front of me. I'm pretty sure that's not how good cop, bad cop is supposed to work! What was particularly disappointing was that they did far too much talking and cutting each other off, as well as me, when it was my turn to speak.

In the early stages of negotiations, the most important thing is to listen and try to determine the important issues of your counterpart. This is critical so that you can determine what is important to them and then you can match your issues with theirs. Once you know all the issues, you can start to bargain and trade for things. But, when your counterpart views you simply as a hostage taker, it's much more difficult.

From my perspective, these two were all about demanding and not giving and that was going to make my job much more difficult. I also didn't get the sense that they knew how this type of negotiation was supposed to work. Theirs was an "all or nothing" mentality.

On my third day in Ottawa, I was contacted by Sgt. Phong Le about an intersection being blocked by us at Bank and Albert, just a few blocks to the West of the Arc Hotel. He wanted me to get at least one lane cleared for EMS. For some reason, instead of sending Mike Stack to go look, which was often the case, I decided to go look for myself.

It was late afternoon and the sun had already gone down. As I walked in that direction, there was a pickup truck burning rubber in the middle of the intersection. The cloud of smoke was ridiculous, and the entire action was unnecessary. While good for the morale of those enjoying the show, it was completely counterproductive in terms of gaining the cooperation of the OPS or any other stakeholder. As I got past the smoke and walked one block north to the intersection, Sgt. Le had been talking about, it was immediately obvious to me that we were not the ones blocking the intersection. It was the City and OPS.

There were concrete jersey barriers, two large pieces of heavy equipment and five OPS Officers all standing there, blocking the intersection and our people were a block south. I returned to the Arc Hotel and was getting the impression that the OPS were just trying to test my behavior and level of cooperation.

The next day, Sgt. Le called me to see if I had cleared the intersection for him as he had asked. I can't speak to his reaction when I informed him that it was his guys blocking the intersection and not us, but I politely reminded him that this was about building a working relationship and that I wasn't there to play any games. At one point in the conversation, I said to him, "You guys keep making demands on us but keep in mind, I haven't asked for anything from you yet." Interestingly his response was "I know." I continued with, "There's going to be a time, in the very near future, when I do." But, when I figured out that one of the tactics they were using was to just show up, at all hours of the day to talk to me, I started to believe that they were just trying to interrupt my day. I didn't know if it was on purpose or just how it was unfolding for them on their end. But, as much as I respected their position and what they were trying to do, my frustration with them had grown more and more.

I had finally told the OPP that I was trained in negotiations and was growing very frustrated with the two OPS Liaison Officers I was dealing with. I had also informed the OPP that I was no longer interested in talking to the OPS Liaison Officers and I insisted that I would only communicate with an Inspector, as a minimum-ranking police officer from the OPS.

Unfortunately, this never happened in the way I was expecting. The next day, I was notified that the OPS would like to have a meeting and I agreed to meet with an Inspector. I had told the Liaison Officer that I wanted ten minutes alone, one-on-one with their Inspector. I arrived at the meeting place ahead of time and was waiting alone in the conference room. To my disappointment, I could hear one of the Liaison Officers telling our people outside the door that there was no way their Inspector would ever meet with me alone. Curious, I went outside the room to see who was there and to my frustration, they didn't bring an Inspector with them. So, without saying a word to them, I walked away and went to my next meeting. I could hear one of them telling me not to leave, but if they wanted to test me this was it. I wasn't phased by it, but I needed to demonstrate my willingness to push back if they didn't show even small concessions. It was just one more demonstration that they were not taking us seriously. This wouldn't be the first time I would walk out of a meeting with these two Liaison Officers.

With one exception, the highest-ranking police officer any of us ever spoke to, was a Sergeant. In fact, the highest-ranking official we ever spoke to was the City Manager, Steve Kanellakos.

Ironically, we didn't directly ask for a meeting with him. The OPS offered it to me, and I later learned that then-Deputy Chief, Steve Bell was involved in arranging that meeting. To be clear, I never asked for a meeting with Steve Kanellakos, but I was happy we did meet.

It was only unelected officials that engaged with us, not the politicians who created this mess, to begin with. It was the largest protest in decades, and no elected official ever spoke to any of us for any level of reasonable dialogue.

One of the most frustrating realizations I had to repeatedly listen to during the POEC, was that no elected official, at any level of government, ever considered talking to us. During the POEC, every time a new government witness was on the stand, I asked Brendan Miller, the lead lawyer representing the Freedom Convoy, to ask the witness if they had ever considered talking to us, instead of immediately defaulting to enforcement action using the police.

Brendan, for tactical reasons, declined to ask the witnesses this question and I had to be quiet and trust he knew what he was doing. At one point during the POEC, Brendan and Keith sat me down calmly and explained what was relevant to the POEC and what wasn't. Bath-Shéba Vandenberg, Brenden's co-council, had also previously tried to explain this to me, but I apparently slept through the day we spoke about Section 2 of the CSIS Act, in Bath-Shéba's law school!

Chapter 9

Mission Command

When I first arrived at the Convoy, I expected that I would stay a few days, help with a good sustainment plan, then go home. I figured I'd find someone to hand it off to and they would keep it going. One of the things I needed to do was create an organizational structure that was really easy to follow and even easier to implement. In NATO militaries, we all use a continental system to get organized and in the case of the Army we have a prefix of 'G' for ground. So, for example, G2 is Intelligence, G3 is known as the Current Operations, G4 is Logistics, G5 is Future

Plans, and G6 is Communications. There are also specialist advisors like legal, aka JAG, but in our case, we had some awesome civilian lawyers from a few different places.

While I was not trying to put together a military unit, I had to structure something fast to divide the duties and responsibilities into easier chunks and this was the system I was most comfortable and experienced with.

On about the fifth day I was there, I was introduced to an awesome guy named Jeff Bouvine, who had a lot of experience in the rail industry. We did a ten second interview in the lobby and I knew he would be a real asset, so I asked him to help and he was eager to get involved. My initial hope was that Jeff could be my number two and would take over from me after a few days.

Jeff is a people person and always kept morale up. He always looked at you and would jokingly say, “I appreciate you.” and you couldn’t help but smile. Jeff was more valuable working on immediate issues as they came up and he’d solve those problems with his own initiative.

The next day we started to relocate our meetings to the two conference rooms on the second floor of the Arc Hotel. I wanted to turn one room into an Operations (Ops) Center and was going to rearrange the desks and assign seating based on the order of the ‘G’ number I was trying to build. I asked Jeff to help me build an organization chart, based on the Army system. At first, Jeff wasn’t too enthusiastic about it, feeling that the span of control was too complicated for everyone to follow. From an outsider’s point of view, I can see why it looked much more complicated than it is.

Jeff accounted for a few positions in the chart that I didn't and in particular he had properly identified housekeeping. I don't mean people who cleaned up after us. I mean people who literally helped us run the Ops Center. All I know is that an amazing married couple, Vickie and Mike, took on this role and made life so much better for all of us. I can't underestimate the value of what they did. On paper, it might seem like a small deal to make sure everything was tidy, or that the photocopier was full of paper, but so many little jobs needed attention. If it wasn't for people like them taking care of all that, we'd have to spend a lot of valuable time doing it ourselves. It was a thankless job, and they did it without ego or complaint. What is amazing is that I found out they were very successful ranchers from the West, and they didn't complain about keeping the Ops Center tidy or the coffee pot going. Absolutely selfless.

It was very typical for highly successful people, to be at the Convoy, and do any job that needed to be done, regardless of who they were back home. One such amazing French-Canadian woman, living in western Canada, was Chantel. She collected people's clothes and did laundry for whoever needed it. At first, I was too embarrassed to let her do this for me because it was my responsibility, but she convinced me to let her help. I have to say, it was an incredible act of kindness, and I was very humbled by it.

One of the positions I was hoping to fill with an experienced person, was our G2 Intelligence role. I made some calls to find someone and was put in contact with Vince Gircys, a well-experienced, retired OPP Officer with over thirty years of service.

In my first conversation with Vince, I needed to be clear with him, that I would never ask him to provide details of a confidential nature about police capabilities. I did not want to put him in a morally difficult position, where he would have to divulge classified or confidential information about the police. I felt that any such attempt would be unnecessary and highly inappropriate. I discussed the same issue with Danny Bulford at a later time. We were not in a life-and-death situation in Ottawa. We were there for a peaceful protest and putting former police officers in a position where they would feel like they may be required to betray their former colleagues was unacceptable to me. It was enough that they were there for personal reasons, and I had to trust they would know they were walking a fine line in some cases. I left it to them to decide what was appropriate to share in terms of how to protect ourselves.

What I was hoping for was that Vince could fill in as G2 and also assist in helping synthesize future plans as G5, if required. The G2 and G5 positions are usually two different people, but I tried not to overcomplicate things. I was going to be heavily involved in any of those discussions as well, for obvious reasons. Again, I wasn't trying to build an army for combat operations, I just wanted to get organized and efficient and build a team of the best, most experienced people. Our highest priority was always to be lawful and safe, as much as possible. Having experienced people in law enforcement was such an incredible asset toward achieving this.

It was in conversations with Vince and some others, that I learned about "kettling" operations and how the police would start to box us in, to make it easier for them to do mass arrests. We noticed the police had set up fences, right on the open grounds of Parliament Hill, and this started to get people a little concerned.

Rumors started to spread like wildfire, which only heightened the level of paranoia that was creeping into our everyday business.

If it wasn't paranoia about the police, it was paranoia about the military being called in. Oftentimes, our people would get panicked and very excited about some rumor they heard. At least twice a day I'd have to tell someone to relax. My catchphrase became "Take a breath, we don't have any Emergency. The only people who do, are police, fire, and ambulance. We have all the time in the world." Then, I would get them to walk me through their dilemma, which after saying it out loud, usually resulted in the person realizing it wasn't as big a deal as they first thought.

However, sometimes the paranoia and rumors were legitimate. For example, we had been told that the police were bringing in special equipment to process a large number of protesters once arrested, at a facility in the suburb of Lansdowne. A team from the Convoy went out to the location where we believed this was going to take place, but the details were very inconclusive and we didn't know for sure if they were going to process us there.

Another thing we had been told was that if they started moving in and making mass arrests, the authorities would jam our internet signals and we wouldn't be able to tell our supporters what was happening. Together with the fences being erected and the information about the processing center being set up, it started looking like the police were getting ready to execute a plan to make arrests. This in addition to what had happened at Coventry the night before led us to believe that we had to do something.

I felt it was important to take action to slow the police down, so on the evening of February 10th, we held a live stream from the Arc Hotel. My intent was to communicate to our supporters, how they could help us if the kettling operations started. I was also trying to communicate to the police that we could potentially delay their attempts to route us out of the city – in a non-physical way. In reality, we knew they could take us at almost anytime and if we were going to stay true to our convictions and not resist, it wouldn't take very long for them to execute their plan of mass arrests.

During the live stream I stated that we believed the police were going to start the kettling operations and that if it appeared to be happening, to come to Ottawa. I said if there was a social media blackout blocking communications from Convoy members, they would know the police were jamming our signals and rounding us up. While I did not say to come to Ottawa immediately, I did ask that they start making arrangements to come if they didn't hear from any of us on social media. It was pre-emptive in nature, but we realized that when the Police were done with their planning, they were going to likely come for us all. Jamming our internet would have been largely to buy themselves time to disrupt our ability to organize any response to the arrests. In truth, I also anticipated they would block the major access routes into the city, for anyone traveling to Ottawa to help us. But, I never discounted the power of good, or bad luck, where the police could have made mistakes that we could take advantage of!

I was feeling I was getting spread too thin, and I needed to find someone who spoke my language in terms of the military shorthand. Six months before the Convoy, a friend of mine, Roberto, introduced me to a guy named Decks, who was a recently retired Naval Officer. Decks was completely disenfranchised by what he believed to be "the managed decline of the Canadian Armed Forces" because they adopted woke policies that prioritized social issues over training.

On the Sunday that Coventry was raided, I messaged Decks and asked him if he could get to Ottawa and if so, how soon could he be there? I wanted Decks because he was highly experienced and a natural leader that others would follow. Most importantly, we spoke the same language and would be mission-focused at all times. People who are like Decks, know how to immediately filter out the noise and not get distracted by irrelevant issues that don't meet the overall objectives. He agreed to come to Ottawa and said the earliest he could be there was on Thursday.

The Canadian military is incredibly small and what makes it such an effective fighting force is that using personal initiative is the very foundation of its success. Our military doesn't have the numbers to specialize, so every member, regardless of branch, trade, or rank, must do more with less. The way this is done is through personal initiative at all rank levels. You can't just wait around to be told what to do every minute of the day. You must see problems and solve them without being directed and you must anticipate what your boss needs to have completed, without being told to do it.

By extension, we take this to a higher level when delivering or receiving formal orders. In NATO countries, a philosophy of leadership is used, known as Mission Command. Again, this is to facilitate maximum initiative at all levels. You are always told your boss's intent and his boss's intent. You must know what each commander, one and two levels above you, "intends" to achieve. We do this so that if your boss is killed or injured, and you get a battlefield promotion, you know what to do. Also, your boss doesn't have to micromanage each phase of the mission and dictate what needs to be done every second. This is where subordinates use their initiative to accomplish the tasks that meet the commander's intent. Lastly, when people know what needs to be done and are allowed to determine how they are done, and in the most effective way, it facilitates creative solutions and allows problems to be solved them to solve problems more freely. In the Convoy, creative problem-solving was vital.

Luckily, instead of getting to Ottawa on Thursday, Decks arrived in the afternoon on Tuesday, February 8th. That was a very busy day, but I was grateful he arrived early so I could brief him on the situation. I really needed a person like Decks to take over the "down and in", meaning the day-to-day stuff because my role was evolving towards the "up and out" strategy. I couldn't effectively do both, so having him there took a load off of me. Initially, I wanted Jeff to do this, but I very quickly realized that Jeff was so good interpersonally that he was better suited to do that face-to-face work directly with the Truckers on the street. He could have easily handled the Ops Room stuff, but his strength of character and motivation was needed more on the streets talking to Truckers.

Talk about personal initiative, when I walked into the Ops Room, Decks was already settled in and had been working on stuff for over an hour, figuring out who the right people were, and I hadn't even briefed him yet! We did the normal greetings and grabbed a coffee at one of the tables.

When we sat down, it was incredibly easy to use a "mission command" approach for my briefing with Decks. I think our meeting was about fifteen minutes max and I can attest to the fact that Decks took in everything he needed to know because I was working with someone who understood my intent.

My intent was derived from my three priorities: first, as many trucks as possible on Wellington; second, morale; and third, social media. I also conveyed to him that we were having a really difficult challenge with communications and it was having a very negative effect on morale. I needed him to make it a priority issue and he absolutely did. Once he understood this, I had to get out of his way and let him run the day-to-day operations in support of the intent to meet these priorities. I need to emphasize that I had to get out of his way and not micromanage the details of how he employed the team to do this. Because I couldn't ask my civilian friends to accept this philosophy and I didn't have time to train them, I asked another military person to come help me, and it worked out perfectly. As time when on, we started to accumulate more veterans and they stuck to a mission command approach.

I have to add one caveat to this. Since we did not have any actual authority over anyone, we had to be mindful that we were not in the military anymore and that our people skills had to get us through this, not barking orders. Decks did exceptionally well at this and proved himself to be a solid leader that people followed. I was thrilled he was there and I trusted he would do what needed to be done, while I started to focus more on the strategic direction with the Board and legal team.

As time went on, we accumulated more former military members, like Eddie Cornell, who I met through Vince Gircys, as well as others.

Chapter 10

Moving Trucks, Conspiracies and Wild Goose Chases

On February 8, 2022, I was asked by Sgt. Le to come to City Hall for a special meeting with a high-ranking authority at approximately 1 p.m. However, it was on the condition that I first move trucks out of the intersection at Rideau Street and Sussex Drive, in front of the Fairmount Chateau Laurier Hotel, on our eastern flank of Wellington. When he first made the request, I told him I didn't make the final decisions, the Freedom Corp. Board did, and that I could only make recommendations. I also committed to trying to convince them to move because to me, he was helping us put trucks exactly where we wanted them, on Wellington, right in front of the Parliament Buildings. I had made it clear to the Board, on several occasions before the 8th, that I was very uneasy with the lack of trucks on Wellington St. and they understood that Wellington needed to be infilled whenever, and however possible. The Truckers I had been surrounded by, understood that too. Also, the Board generally understood that we all needed to do what we could, to bring the temperature down.

I began the early morning with a meeting of the truck Captains, in the main conference room on Wellington. Jeff Bouvine had started the meeting and the room was almost packed. Unfortunately, not everyone in the meeting spoke English so there had to be a translator. This is the day that I met some of the most hardcore Truckers in the Convoy. The guys from Quebec! While they were there as part of the Convoy, they had arrived as a separate entity the night before the main body had arrived on the 28th of January. It was known that they would work with us, but it was clear they made their own decisions independent from us. Since I often struggled to leave the Arc Hotel, I hadn't interacted with them directly until this day.

This was day eleven for me in Ottawa, and we had been working extremely hard to solve our communications problem with all the Truckers. Messages were still not getting out to everyone. Again, a lack of information was contributing to the morale being eroded daily, and Truckers were starting to leave faster than new trucks were arriving to replace them. Or so it seemed.

As Jeff was doing his opening remarks, it seemed to be going on for much longer than anticipated and the room itself was starting to really heat up. On average, humans give off about 100 watts of heat, so in a full room of people wearing warm outdoor clothing, it didn't take long for that room to start cooking.

There were so many new faces for me, I realized that most people there had no idea who I was. When it was my time to speak, I started with, "How many people in this room have no clue who I am?" From the count, I estimated that about 75% of the room had no idea. Then I realized, I'd been there for eleven days and no one on the streets knew there was a team inside the Arc Hotel, trying to make this work. It wasn't just me they didn't know; it was many of us.

After I did a quick intro about myself, our purpose, and what we had been doing, I addressed the issue of low morale among the Truckers. I had been hearing rumors of Truckers leaving in the middle of the night because they didn't know what was happening and they were growing frustrated. I needed to say something to these people to convince them we were working on a plan and to also inspire some personal responsibility.

As I stood in front of this room of patriotic Canadians, my instinct was to go with a little tough-love approach. I sympathized with the personal discomfort living in their Trucks, but also quoted a saying from the US Navy SEALS, "The only easy day was yesterday." I further went on to say, "As each day away from home passes, your comfort is going to get just a little harder, and it will be harder to stay than the day before." I knew I needed to manage expectations but not allow boredom to get the better of them and their imaginations, with all the rumors flying around. I addressed the communications problem we were having and took responsibility for information not being shared with them, but I also said they had to accept a measure of responsibility for it too. At one point, I said, "If you see someone in their truck feeling sorry for themself, tell them that this isn't the place to do it. You can't feel sorry for yourself sitting in your trucks now when two years from now you might be sitting by yourself in a Covid camp against your will. This is it; this is the line in the sand we all drew and we won't ever get a second chance to be heard." For the most part, they got it.

Before I finished my talking points, I had one more thing to tell them, but the room was getting unbearably hot. The length of my talk was extended because I had to keep stopping to allow for French translations.

I informed them that the police wanted us to move out of the Rideau and Sussex intersection and that we were going to try to do that if possible, in exchange for moving them further west onto Wellington.

This was when I first met Guillaume. He was a young and fit, father of two children, one of whom has a new baby back in Quebec. I had never spoken to him before, but he immediately raised his objections to moving out of that intersection. I have to say, I immediately admired this guy, but I had to also argue hard against his perspective. The exchange got a little heated and I yelled, "Do you want to take over? Because if you have a better idea on how to get some negotiations going with the government, let’s hear it! If you think you can do a better job, by all means please take over and I’ll follow you if you have a better plan.” It’s not in my normal character to be aggressive, but I felt the situation required it of me in that moment. I deeply regretted that I had to take this posture with Guillaume, because I could see on his face that he was there for the exact same reasons as me and the rest of the people in the Convoy.

I ended the meeting with the reasoning that it was too hot in the room to stay and keep talking. I did get a few more minutes to talk to Guillaume but the result was the same. We couldn’t agree about moving from the intersection to Wellington, but I had to go because I was going to meet with Sgt. Le at City Hall and didn’t want to be late. I view being late as a sign of disrespect and I didn’t want to start with the wrong tone.

Considering I thought I was going to be arrested by OPS after doing the live stream about their kettling operation, I decided it would be smart to bring Keith and Eva to this meeting, just in case the offer to meet a high-ranking person was a ruse so I would turn myself over to the OPS.

I arrived at the north entrance door and was met by Sgt. Le. To say the conversation got a little awkward was an understatement. His basic stance was, that because I didn’t already get the Truckers to move, he didn’t see why he needed to let the meeting go forward. So, I reminded him that they didn’t work for me or follow orders like soldiers. He also didn’t seem to have a realistic understanding of how long it would take them to move, that’s if they decided to do so, given that there were concrete barriers blocking trucks, and OPS cars everywhere.

Additionally, he said to me, “If you can’t get them to move, why should I even talk to you anymore?” My response was to reciprocate his attitude and let him know that I didn’t want to deal with him anymore regardless.

As that conversation was taking place, Keith and Eva arrived but were a little late because I hadn’t told them what door to go to. When Sgt. Le saw Keith and Eva, he was irritated by that too, because he wasn’t expecting to see two lawyers attending with me.

During the POEC, we heard testimony that it was Deputy Chief Steve Bell, who arranged for that meeting to go forward between us and the city. I just happened to be the Convoy representative the OPS identified as the one to have the meeting. Although on the 7th, I had publicly called for a meeting with the city, this was how they were responding.

From all Sgt. Le’s blustering in the moment and from my previous dealings with him, I lost even more confidence in continuing to discuss it further and considered walking away altogether. To be clear, that was when I found out who I was meeting with, and meeting the City Manager was significant. I just didn’t want to give Sgt. Le the impression that I was desperate and instead tried to convey an uninterested posture. Thanks to Eva and her calm demeanor, she saved the situation. Sgt. Le made a cell phone call and the meeting was allowed to go forward as planned. The goal was to always de-escalate tensions but sometimes it was just really difficult with Sgt. Le.

We were escorted upstairs to enter the executive wing of the building. OPP Constable Andrew Wierzbicki, whom I came to admire because of his outstanding professionalism, was also there. He was with an OPS Constable named Isabelle. My dealings with her were few so I don't recall her last name, but many people who dealt with her, held her in high regard. As she wore a mask, she was very difficult for me to read, but she was always professional.

Strangely, the three of us were frisked and we were made to leave our cell phones in our coats in the outer hallway. I wondered if it was just an intimidation tactic, but clearly, that kind of thing doesn't work on people like us. Did they think two lawyers and a retired army guy were a serious threat to anyone?

As we made our way inside the mayor's wing of City Hall, I asked Keith and Eva to remain outside because I wanted to go in and talk to Steve Kanellakos alone for a few minutes. Without question, both Keith and Eva understood my intention for doing that. We all knew that if I had not been the first person in that room, Steve would have most likely just dealt with the lawyers and not me. I had to establish myself as a Convoy participant who was getting legal advice from the two lawyers and that the lawyers were not leading the Convoy. Additionally, I always had it in my mind that I needed to protect them from being labeled as organizers of the Convoy. As legal advisors, I felt they needed a measure of separation between themselves and us. The juxtaposition was very important because I also had to convey that we were getting some serious professional advice and that we were acting as legally and responsibly as humanly possible. In absolute truth, they were there providing a critical function for both sides and I didn't want to see them jailed for it. I would have gone to jail for fight for our freedoms, but they should not get punished for helping us stay within legal boundaries.

The other reason I wanted to meet with Steve alone, was to build some trust and rapport and to convey to him that they had someone on our side who was reasonable and focused on the right things. If Tamara and Chris, or any other Board member had been invited, I would have brought them into the meeting with me and Steve as well. I was the guy who got the offer to meet so I wanted to make sure I conveyed the right message.

Steve and I did the usual pleasantries and I reflected on my time in the army when I worked in the Construction Engineers Department, and how his role as a city manager, was very similar to a base commander. I remember him asking me how I got involved in all of this and I told him about getting fired from my job a few months before. I explained what I had been experiencing as an unvaccinated person trying to protect my unvaccinated family. By being reasonable and humanizing my own story, I was trying to build a rapport and determine if he was reasonable and willing to find an amicable solution. Had he shown any ill intent, I would have walked out of that room and not continued with Keith and Eva. To Steve's credit, he is a highly reasonable and professional man who also had a job to do on behalf of his city.

While I was in Steve's office, Keith and Eva were outside building a rapport of their own with the police officers in the hall. I think this was just as important a step as what was happening with me and Steve because the police learned why Keith was also motivated so strongly to be in Ottawa. I won't repeat his story because it is not mine to tell. I will just say it is deeply personal and he is the one who should speak about it himself. In that exchange, Eva felt it was appropriate for Keith to share his experiences with the police officers and he agreed. I didn't know the story myself until the following August.

Keith, Eva, and the rest of the police officers came into the room after my initial conversation with Steve and we quickly summarized the important details. While Steve acknowledged that Canadians had a right to come to their national capital to protest, he expressed to us that the federal government had not provided any support to the city. From his perspective, he wanted to work with us to relieve the pressure on three trouble areas.

Steve stated that the city wanted the trucks out of the residential areas, which they identified as anything south of Wellington. If we did that and restricted our footprint to Wellington, they didn't care how long we stayed. But for them, the three most important areas were Metcalfe Street between Slater and Wellington, Lyon Street between Slater and Wellington, and finally they needed a lane open on Kent Street. They wanted the major streets that are perpendicular to Wellington opened up in these designated residential areas.

Just before we concluded the meeting, Keith asked a very smart question about what to say to the media if we had all been seen walking out of City Hall together. Steve had an interesting facial reaction and realized that this could be troublesome. In reality, it was Keith's subtle way of developing further trust between Steve and us. We agreed we would say we had established a line of communication with the city staff and no more. He couldn't have us doing a press conference in front of

City Hall saying all sorts of things that they would have to deal with.

For us, this would have been incredibly stupid since we were just offered the deal of the century to consolidate all our trucks on Trudeau's doorstep, which is exactly what I wanted from day one! To me, this would have been a monumental win. I just needed to get the Truckers at Sussex and Rideau to agree to move – and I knew it was going to be next to impossible, under the best of conditions!

During the POEC, I learned that the OPS had two Deputy Chiefs of Police. Deputy Chief Steve Bell and newly promoted Deputy Chief Patricia Ferguson, who had very significant experience working with Police Liaison Teams. She testified about the command structure during the POEC, and that there had been significant changes in leadership of the "Event Commander". Initially it was Superintendent Rheaume but then quickly changed to Superintendent Dunlop from February 4th to the evening of the 5th. Chief Sloly felt that Superintendent Dunlop was not the right person for that job and subsequently replaced him with Superintendent Mark Patterson from February 6th only to February 10th. Deputy Chief Ferguson did not agree with this decision, as it undermined her authority to select the Event Commander. However, because there was a personal issue between Chief Sloly and Superintendent Dunlop, she relented with consultation from Deputy Chief Bell. Superintendent Mark Patterson was then replaced by Superintendent Bernier after February 10th. From the 28th of January to the 10th of February, there had been four different Event Commanders assigned to deal with the largest protest in the city's history!

It was Deputy Chief Ferguson's responsibility, as the "Major Incident Commander" to convey strategic direction to the Event Commander. The Event Commander assigns the task of making a tactical plan and then is the approving authority for that plan.

After the first weekend, on Monday, January 31st, the OPS refocused their thinking and started viewing the Freedom Convoy as an "occupation" instead of a protest. This new perspective shaped their new planning framework. As of the 4th of February, the OPS had developed a loose plan based on priorities set by Police Chief, Peter Sloly. It was interesting that it was seen by many in the senior leadership team of the OPS, that Chief Sloly was directing operational plans, which was contrary to their Incident Command Model of delegating decisions down to lower levels. Deputy Chief Ferguson testified that Chief Sloly had to be reminded his role was not to direct police operations, because he was getting too far down into the details and talking directly to constables.

As of the 5th of February, Chief Sloly had set certain general priorities. One: "Surge, contain, and enforce". The second being, "Close off everything: roads, bridges, and highways - as early and as long as possible." The third priority, to shut down several things, like the funds, the fundraising, the fuel, and shut down the fun. He also itemized priorities regarding specific locations. It was Chief Sloly's intention to see Confederation Park, the Rideau/Sussex intersection, the Sir John A. MacDonald Parkway, and Wellington Street, all shut down completely.

Deputy Chief Ferguson testified during the POEC, that when Superintendent Patterson took over as the Event Commander on the 6th, he was going to get some "wins" by implementing a plan to meet Chief Sloly's strategic priorities. This issue however, was completely counterproductive in the view of the OPS and OPP Police Liaison Team efforts this far in the protest. There were internal OPS discussions advocating for the PLT to have more time to de-escalate any potential issues at Coventry and if the results were not proving successful, then the POU could be used as a more direct approach with arrests of protesters. This was also the recommended approach by the OPP.

However, when Superintendent Patterson made the decision to send the POU to raid Coventry on the evening of the 6th, it created a very tense working relationship between the PLT from both the OPS and OPP with the Event Commander. Patterson did not even inform the PLTs that he was sending in the POU. This aggressive action by Patterson was seen as a betrayal by the PLT Officers who had been trying so diligently to work with all of us, which for them was yielding some good results.

For example, PLT Officers were successful at clearing out a section of Confederation Park through an engagement strategy, that was safe for everyone involved. It did not require the aggressive, surge, contain, and enforce strategy that Chief Sloly had been pushing.

After the Coventry raid, by the POU, their credibility, from our perspective was greatly diminished and it impacted relations with the PLTs. What was interesting is that Chief Sloly was aware that they could lose PLT support from the OPP by using the POU in Coventry the way they did.

From my perspective, I saw it as an opportunity we could hopefully exploit. I was hoping they would now come to us, with an offer of some kind, because I knew they had made a major blunder with the Coventry raid. So, just to be sure, I did my livestream the next day on the 7th.

After leaving the meeting with Steve Kanellakos, we decided that Eva, Keith, and I would head to the intersection of Sussex and Rideau. Given that the city would have to get involved by moving concrete barriers, in our view we were carrying out directions that had already been well established by the Board and we didn't want to delay getting the trucks moved. Keith returned to the Sheraton to work on other issues we had going on. If we had a difficult time, we knew we would be able to get Keith to come back and help us out with the Truckers or the OPS, at that intersection.

I spent some time walking around and looking at the layout of the intersection and how the Truckers had spread themselves out. This area is a convergence of several different streets. At one point I was speaking with one of the Truckers who was carrying a brown paper bag that contained letters from families around the country. He had been collecting the letters and keeping them to share the stories with people. He told me about his friend whose six-year-old daughter had been suicidal because of the toll the lockdowns and masks had been having on her. The letters in the bag were filled with these types of stories from around the country.

During my conversation with him, I noticed the intersection was blocked three lanes across and we spoke about my concern for getting safety vehicles through the intersection. What I learned, is what informed me of the justifiable mistrust the Truckers had for the police. I was told that in the early days of their arrival, the OPS would trick them into moving their trucks, stating they had to move for safety reasons, only to have the police move right into their spots with their cars. After the third incident of this, they decided they'd had enough. When I asked him about emergency vehicles, he told me they always manned the trucks in one lane and listened for sirens. When they heard them, they moved just enough to let the emergency vehicles through and then quickly returned to the original spots. He assured me that this is what they had done on two separate occasions, and it worked for them.

I learned it was widely believed the city wanted the trucks moved because a billionaire owned all the property around that intersection, and he was putting pressure on the mayor. I was also told the mayor lived there and didn't like it. Another concern the Truckers had, was they believed Wellington to be federal property and that those who were on federal property could be charged with a federal crime. The irony was no one seemed to know who had jurisdiction over Wellington. Prior to the POEC, we heard there was confusion between the OPS and the PPS as to which Police department had jurisdiction over Wellington. To me, it didn't matter if these things were true, or not. What mattered was that we would never get anywhere if we were not able to take the pressure off the city.

The Truckers at this intersection were not just from the Quebec side. There was also a Polish-Canadian contingent, as well as Truckers from a few different provinces. However, it was clear to me that the French Truckers had the greatest influence over everyone at that intersection.

I can't understand how it happened, but after my walk around, and Eva's conversations with the Polish Truckers, she and I ended up in a large pickup truck with Guillaume, who I had the argument with earlier that morning. I was seated up front on the passenger side and Eva was in the backseat. We also met another French-Canadian named Norm. There were definitely challenges with language. Norm's English was better than Guillaume's, but my French is horrific, so we had to make it work in English.

A major issue besides the language barrier, was the fact that both guys were chain smokers and I had been dealing with a brutal chest cold I picked up from Chris Barber the day after I arrived, so it was tough to stay in Guillaume's truck.

I knew it was only a matter of time until I got that cold. I started to feel sick and had a crashing headache, then unbelievable night sweats. I experienced the sorest throat of my life and eventually, the cough came. As I mentioned, Dr. Rodger Hodkinson, who had done some hilarious hallway medicine at the Arc Hotel, said it was likely the Omicron strain of Covid-19. I was certainly not 100% the entire time I was in Ottawa, but it didn't stop me from doing my job!

During that two-hour conversation, I learned more about

Guillaume's situation and that he was also there for his kids. I had absolutely no doubt that he was committed to staying in Ottawa for as long as it took to stop all of the federal mandates. We rehashed the same arguments we had in the morning, but I wasn't convincing him as to why we should move off of the intersection and onto Wellington. Eva was also doing her best and I could tell that he was more inclined to listen to her, not just because she's persuasive but because she is a lawyer. He also repeated the story about the billionaire and the mayor, and the subject of the US Embassy came up as well. I knew the US Embassy staff would not have been comfortable, given the history of US Embassies around the globe, but they were not my concern in terms of what I was trying to do. I could sense Norm was more willing to consider moving off the intersection. I think he realized it was pointless to stay there forever without trying to get a negotiation with the government and that it wouldn't happen without helping the city too.

There had always been concern that moving from the intersection onto Wellington, weakened our position. I had considered that, in the very first hours of being in Ottawa. Yes, from a tactical strategy, this was a weaker position in terms of the POU doing their kettling operation and making it easier to round us all up. However, this was not a combat situation and we had always advocated for peaceful protesting, not violent action. So, in my estimation, tactics were less important to me than having a strategic plan. To me, we had to be parked right on the doorstep of Parliament so they couldn't ignore us. As long as we remained peaceful, they'd have to talk to us eventually. Concurrently we had a highly effective social media campaign, which was going exceptionally well, given that we had raised millions of dollars from donors around the country.

Before we could move any of the trucks onto Wellington, the city would have to move the concrete barriers they put between the intersection and Wellington, further west.

As it started to get darker outside, I convinced Norm and Guillaume to talk it over with everyone on the intersection and to elect two of them to talk with me and the PLTs who were there. Sgt. Le was the main PLT Officer I was dealing with and I was concerned about him. I had already seen him interact with a room full of Truckers in my first five minutes of being at the Convoy and he tended to talk aggressively at times. Sgt. Le came close to where I was talking to the Truckers, and it gave me a very bad vibe. I didn't want Sgt. Le standing in the center of a large group that we estimated to be about seventy-five Truckers. Given his personality, I just didn't feel good about him standing by himself in the middle of these agitated men.

I had gone to Sgt. Le and told him that I asked the Truckers to decide on two people who would speak for them and then we'd all have a meeting. As I was talking to Sgt. Le, his cell phone rang and he walked away from me. Behind me were the Truckers, who were deciding who was going to meet with the PLTs, and in front of me I had Sgt. Le who was now on the phone and walking away from me.

As Sgt. Le finished his phone call, he turned toward me, and I immediately knew that both he and I just got screwed completely by his OPS chain-of-command. I could see on his face that he was upset and frustrated. I walked toward him to get out of earshot of the Truckers and find out what was happening. Sgt. Le was now in a tough spot. He had been trying to get the intersection cleared out since the day before, using the same method as they did at Confederation Park. When we had all finally got to the five-yard-line, his own police leadership pulled the carpet out from under us all. I knew it wasn't his fault and he was trying to save face and cover for the OPS. Regrettably, instead of being honest, he lied to me and said the deal was not to move trucks onto Wellington, but for us to leave the downtown core altogether. He stated it as though it was a miscommunication between us. I believe it was a deliberate miscommunication with the OPS leadership and him.

Unfortunately, Eva and I had just spent the afternoon trying to convince the Truckers to move and they were willing to at least discuss it with the OPS. But now I had a new problem.

I couldn't go back to the Truckers and tell them that their time and energy had been completely wasted. They didn't want to move to begin with and now the deal was called off. To them, it would have been just another example of why they shouldn't trust the OPS or any other Police department. As the two selected Truckers came toward me, thinking they would be talking to the OPS, I intercepted them instead so they wouldn't have to hear the news from Sgt. Le. Before I told them, I told Sgt. Le that I was going to use the excuse that it was too dark to move the concrete barriers and then reposition large trucks. That would at least be a reasonable explanation as to why we were calling off the move that evening, but the Truckers were already suspicious of the OPS and this did further damage to their credibility.

Superintendent Rob Drummond testified at the POEC, that it was Superintendent Mark Patterson who asked Deputy Chief Bell to arrange a meeting between Steve Kanellakos and one of us. What was most troubling about this entire event was that the day before I was offered to meet with Steve Kanellakos, Superintendent Mark Patterson, as the delegated Event Command authority, had predetermined that we would not be allowed to move the trucks onto Wellington. Not only did he undermine me in the eyes of the most difficult group of Truckers, he weakened the credibility of the OPS-PLT Officers for a second time in two days.

Truthfully, I didn't care that Sgt. Le lied to me in order to be loyal to his boss. What upset me was that he thought I was stupid enough to have fallen for it in the first place.

The next day Keith, Eva, and I met with Sgt. Le, Sgt. Carvello, and Constable Andrew Wierzbicki from the OPP at the Sheraton. The intent of the meeting was to see what we could do to resolve the situation from the afternoon before and get trucks moved onto Wellington again. In a strange twist, Sgt. Le accused me of misunderstanding what had happened, saying that I knew the original deal was to have the trucks move out of the city, and not onto Wellington. For me, being called a liar by Sgt. Le was beyond frustrating and I didn't think the OPS was in a position to be calling anyone's actions into question.

In that moment, I knew dealing with him directly was an absolute waste of my time and energy. When you realize you're not dealing with someone who is interested in working with you to solve problems, you move on until you find someone who is.

Instead of having any form of rebuttal with Sgt. Le, I decided the smartest option was to leave. So, I stood up, grabbed my coat, and walked out of the room without saying a word. I also wanted those police officers to know I wasn't afraid of them and that I wouldn't be pushed around by anyone. When you play stupid games, you win stupid prizes. I had reached the limit of patience with a PLO who didn't recognize I was trying to help him work toward the same goals. His 'winner takes all' approach was inappropriate and unnecessary.

I later reconnected with Keith and Eva to go over what happened after I left the meeting. We had all agreed that my departure from the meeting was the right move because it allowed Keith and Eva to do a good cop, bad cop routine, on the cops! However, Keith was scheduled for a live interview with Fox News and had to leave shortly. But, he didn't leave the meeting before making sure he let the Police know that he was about to go live on Fox News. Clearly, they understood he had an opportunity to go on international television to talk about what happened the day before as well as what just happened in the meeting I had walked out of.

Before Keith left he suggested that the protestors have the ability to call in three more protestors for every one OPS arrested. After Keith was gone, one of the police stated to Eva, "You can play the tit-for-tat game."

According to Eva, she responded with, "What did you say about tit for tat?" And he repeated it. Eva replied, leaning in toward them with finger pointing. "Don't talk to us about tit for tat. You stole the fuel from protesters. There was no tat. You beat up an elderly man. There was no tat. You are constantly playing games with the protestors, reneging on agreements, and there's been no tat. So don't talk about tit-for-tat to me." The police definitely saw a different side of Eva!

If the plan to get more trucks onto Wellington was approved, Sgt. Le wanted confirmation about how many trucks would move. Eva advised him that they were all independent Truckers. She firmly told them that the Truckers needed honesty from the police as it would not instill confidence in the designated "leaders" if the deals were reneged on, by the OPS. She explained to them that stealing food and fuel and beating up old men does not encourage cooperation and instill trust.

Eva was referring to a video that went viral of an elderly protester being physically manhandled by a younger OPS Officer, as he was being arrested. The video made people extremely upset and trust was rapidly deteriorating. Keith and Eva reaffirmed that the Truckers wanted to work with authorities and the city to mitigate impacts, but the city needed to work with the Truckers, not against them.

At the conclusion of the meeting, Sgt. Le said he would advise us if he was given authority by the Event Commander, Superintendent Patterson, to move the concrete barriers and allow the trucks to move onto Wellington. Concurrently, Eva agreed to get the ball rolling in terms of preparing the Truckers for the move.

Easier said than done!

The next day, on the morning of the 10th,, Eva organized a

meeting with the Freedom Corp. Board, at Rideau and Sussex, to speak with the Truckers and again convince them to move the trucks onto Wellington. Unfortunately, there was a delay as Sgt. Le didn't have authorization as yet from the OPS. Again, another standstill between the Convoy and OPS.

However, at one point, the OPS spoke to Tamara and Chris about a specific large semi they had attempted to move from a very awkward position in front of the Chateau Laurier. Thankfully, Chris Barber was able to have the truck moved into an acceptable new position.

Then at approximately 4 p.m. Sgt. Le stated he had the go-ahead to move the concrete barriers, so we could finally proceed with the plan we had been working on for two days. Unfortunately, there was no prior notice or warning that this was about to happen, even while it was getting dark. The Board members tried to convince the Truckers to move but there was a lot of confusion about what was going on.

When the police finally brought in the equipment to move the concrete barriers it was very dark and all of the supporters who were there, assumed the police were about to start clearing out the intersection and making mass arrests.

From my perspective, this was a direct result of the PLT infighting and officers being undermined at every turn, by their own leadership. Also, the actions of the Public Order Unit at Coventry were still very fresh in people's minds.

Hundreds of Ottawa residents encircled the police and started singing "O Canada" and chanting "Shame. Shame. Shame." At one point, Keith sensed that the PLT Officers were now in harm's way and chose to pull them away from the crowd. Again, after a second day of trying, all efforts to move the trucks out of the intersection and onto Wellington had failed.

Chapter 11

The Veterans at the National War Memorial

Prior to the 12th of February, there was a very isolated incident where a young woman was recorded on video, standing on top of the Tomb of the Unknown Soldier, the National War Memorial.

Emotions about this incident ran very high for everyone involved until it was discovered that the woman didn't understand what she was standing on because it was covered with snow. I watched the video myself and you could immediately see that she removed herself from the Tomb as soon as she realized she was standing on something of great significance. All my life I have seen civilians disrespect military monuments, as though they were at a military playground. From what I watched, this was not one of those moments.

There were also complaints about the Terry Fox statue being "desecrated" because someone put a Canadian Flag on him like a cape and another Canadian Flag upside down on a pole as a symbol of distress. There was also a sign put in his arms that said, "Mandate Freedom". Of course, the media and local politicians had a field day with these two incidents.

The City of Ottawa has a long history of the National War Memorial being vandalized and decided to erect a large fence around the Memorial and the Tomb. To the hundreds of veterans in Ottawa, this was unacceptable.

Chris Barber and I had decided to go to Wellington to follow up on the situation with moving the trucks away from the intersection of Rideau and Sussex. As I walked there with Chris, it was like walking down the street with a celebrity. We kept getting stopped along the way by people who wanted to meet him.

As we arrived at the National War Memorial, there were a lot of veterans there in medals, jackets, and berets. It was surprising to see that many people and suddenly there was a lot of commotion as the veterans started to remove the fence around the Memorial.

I thought it was great, but by now I had made myself known publicly and I wanted to be careful. I did not participate in the removal of the fence. I didn't want to draw attention to myself and then have the media attack the veterans for it, because I was there.

As if on cue, a large group of OPS arrived on the scene. They came in very aggressively like they typically do. Once they realized who had removed the fence, the police started discussing the situation with the veterans. There was also a quick and professional dialogue between the veterans about their protecting and maintaining a 24/7 security guard on the Memorial themselves. To the credit of the OPS, they came into the area, vast and decisively, but exited the same way when they realized the veterans were serious about guarding the Memorial.

Jake Spinney, an Afghanistan veteran, was right at the center of the discussions. Jake is built like a modern-day Viking and speaks his mind without hesitation. As I was standing close to the Memorial talking to two other veterans, Eddie Cornell and Padre Harold Ristau, Jake was on one end of a long ice scraper removing all of the snow and ice that had accumulated on the Monument steps.

Padre Ristau commented he wished he was more prepared because he could have done a prayer at the Memorial. I looked at him and Eddie and said, "Do it anyway," and the two of them agreed. Eddie got everyone's attention and Padre Ristau moved up onto the steps that Jake had just cleaned off and began a prayer for all of us.

One of the most inspiring moments of that spontaneous event

was as soon as he finished the prayer, the crowd started to sing "Oh Canada". It was incredibly emotional and more inspiring than any Remembrance Day Ceremony I had ever attended.

Moments later, I was recognized and surrounded by people who wanted to talk about the joy and happiness of what they witnessed firsthand from everyone who participated in the Convoy. Suddenly I heard some intense screaming and so I turned around to see Jake Spinney going on 'full-auto' at some mainstream media reporters. He was telling them to leave and expressing his discontent with their lies over the last two years. Honestly, at the time, I wished I had a hot drink and some popcorn to sit there watching Jake let the media have it.

They deserved it, and there was no way he was going to let them vilify Canadian veterans, on that sacred ground. For the remainder of the protest in Ottawa, Canadian veterans guarded the National War Memorial 24/7.

February 18th was the first day of the attacks by the Police. Chris Deering, a Canadian Army combat veteran, had arrived the afternoon before, after a ten-hour drive all the way from Nova Scotia.

Chris was nearly killed in Afghanistan fourteen years earlier when the LAV-III armored vehicle he was in, drove over an Improvised Explosive Device, or IED. The vehicle was launched 100 feet in the air and two of his comrades were killed instantly. While in the air, the vehicle flipped over and the turret fell out in one direction while Chris was ejected in another. Luckily for

Chris, nothing fell on top of him after he landed on the ground. His injuries were extensive. He suffered severe damage to his back, a broken pelvis, as well as facial fractures, and other injuries, and still has ongoing challenges with his short-term memory.

On the morning of the 18th, Chris was having coffee at about 8 a.m. at the Memorial with a large group of about twenty veterans. At around noon, they noticed a group of police had arrived and formed a line. Some of them, including Chris had a chance to speak with the police and pleaded with them not to do what they were doing to the peaceful protesters. During his conversation with the police, Chris showed them a picture of the crater from the IED, that had almost killed him. He also was identifying himself to them so that if they arrested him, and the others, he hoped they wouldn't be too rough.

After pleading with the police and realizing it was futile, the veterans quickly sorted themselves out and formed a line as well, and linked arms, bracing for imminent arrests. After forty-five minutes linked together and peacefully resisting, Chris just couldn't physically stand up anymore. The police were in contact with the veterans, but it looked more like a rugby scrum than anything that resembled a violent encounter with police.

Finally, Chris just surrendered to the pain of his injuries and allowed the police to take him into custody. Unfortunately for Chris, the police officer he spoke to, didn't care about Chris's injuries. The officer started kneeing him in the ribs and kicking him in the back. Once he was down on the ground trying to protect himself in the fetal position, the officer continued to kick

Chris in the ankle and foot. Chris covered his face and was screaming, “I'm very peaceful. I'm peaceful. I'm not resisting." But the police punched him in the head several times, while he was down.

Chris had his hands zip-tied behind his back while following orders to stand in a line for approximately two hours. He was in excruciating pain and was denied his prescription pain medication by the Police who were running the processing line. During the POEC, Chris testified that it was the worse pain he had experienced since being blown up in Afghanistan.

Once Chris was through the line, after being photographed and charged with mischief, he was loaded into a police car and driven twenty kilometres away from the city and dropped off at an outdoor police compound, without shelter or a cell phone to call for a ride. Luckily for Chris, he wasn’t the only one there. Several other people who had been arrested, including veterans, were just dropped off with no way to get home.

To this day, I can’t comprehend how a police officer in Canada, could obey an order to attack peaceful protesters with such violence and ease. Chris was not the only veteran to be physically beaten by Canadian police. I don’t want to say veterans are better than the average Canadians who were beaten and arrested, but the fact that the veterans have literally given blood for the freedoms of this country, beating them on an order from a scoundrel and coward like Justin Trudeau, is beyond shameful. I hope for the rest of their lives, that every year on Remembrance Day, the police who beat our veterans feel absolute shame for what they did.

Tom Quiggin, wrote some important words, in support of the Dutch Veterans who were also helping their farmers protest. "A veteran can no longer be the tip of the spear, but they can be the shield." On that day, and throughout the Convoy, hundreds of veterans came to Ottawa, feeling duty-bound, to once again be a shield for Canadians.

Chapter 12

Political Games by the Mayor of Ottawa

As early as the 4th of February, we knew the Mayor of Ottawa, Jim Watson, was going to be a problem. Eva had sent a letter to the OPS and the mayor's office requesting the CCTV cameras be turned back on, so the public could see that there were no acts of violence and that crime had been reduced since our arrival.

On the same day, Keith was served a nuisance lawsuit naming

several of the Convoy leadership, including Tamara, Chris, and others. That evening, both Keith and Eva started working on getting affidavits and messages from local residents in support of the Convoy. There was an injunction filed in court, to force the Convoy to stop honking their truck horns. Keith and Eva had to stay up all night because they were expected in Justice McClean's courtroom at 1 p.m. the next day and there was very little time for them to prepare.

They arrived with 200 messages of support from the local residents and thankfully they were granted an adjournment until Monday the 7th. During the court application, which took several hours, Justice McLean granted an injunction for honking. However, paragraph 7 of the court order reads: "THIS COURT ORDERS that, provided the terms of this Order are complied with, the Defendants and other persons remain at liberty to engage in a peaceful, lawful, and safe protest."

For us, this meant we just had a judge rule that our protest was lawful, as long as we stopped honking horns, which was absolutely fine with me and Chris.

Thankfully, after my conversations with Keith about the Police Services Board meeting on the 4th of February, he had seen the same thing I had regarding the pressure on Chief Sloly. On the 6th of February, he started looking for a mediator to help us get something going with the city and he contacted Premier Peckford to see if he knew anyone in Ontario who could assist us. The name he was given was Dean French, who happened to be a former Chief of Staff (COS) to Doug Ford the Premier of Ontario.

One of the things you need to do in negotiations is first have an understanding of who the key players are and find a mediator in cases such as ours. Keith was absolutely right to find someone, and Dean was who we had. In his capacity as COS, Dean had a relationship with the Mayor of Ottawa. We needed someone who had direct access to Watson, and we took what we had. First, you need to back-channel to see if there is even an appetite for the opposing side to hold any form of talks. You don't want to find out publicly, that your opponent won't talk to you and that they will use the opportunity to try to humiliate you. For example, I'd never expect for the Mayor to call me directly on my phone and ask to talk. He wouldn't risk his negotiating position on someone he didn't know. You have to find out if they're willing to talk, so you need a third-party mediator to make future discussions happen. To me, this was Diplomacy 101 and it wasn't complicated. Yet, it would later be misconstrued that we were making deals behind people's backs. We knew we couldn't be in Ottawa forever, so a mediator was essential to get discussions going. That way we could build on those meetings and get to the Liberal government in the future.

Additionally, there was a very influential man in the Peterborough area who also had connections to Dean French. I had never met him, but he was a long-time supporter of the Ontario Conservatives and was appalled by the actions of Doug Ford and the federal government. It was this man who arranged to fly Dean French to Ottawa, in his own plane, to help us negotiate with the city.

The same day the Police raided Coventry, the City of Ottawa declared a State of Emergency and the next day sent a letter to the Prime Minister and Public Safety Minister. The letter stated, "The demonstration has turned into an aggressive and hateful occupation of our neighborhoods." This seemed to be directly opposite to the messages of support from local residents, that Keith and Eva had shown to Justice McLean, the same day.

It wasn't until a few days later, on Friday the 11th, that myself, Keith, Eva, and several members of the Freedom Corp. Board met with Dean French for the first time in person. Dean explained the current thinking of the mayor and his desire to relieve pressure on the residential areas close to Wellington. During that meeting, he shared a letter from Watson, stating that he would like us to move out of the residential areas, in exchange for a meeting with us.

I thought the entire thing was absurd since we had been trying to do that already. But I was willing to play along if it meant we could finally get trucks onto Wellington, which again had been the plan for days.

I was one of the first ones to speak, as I supported this concept for a few reasons, but mainly because it was well within the strategy of concentrating our trucks onto Wellington. Because I was not a member of the Board, I wanted my thoughts to be known before the Board Members in the room started discussing it.

After the Convoy there was growing concern, initiated by a former Board Member who was removed, who started to spread lies that Keith and I did a backroom deal with Dean French. It was ridiculous. Keith had phone conversations and texts with Dean, and the one and only time, I ever met with him was in the room with the Board members present. Additionally, Dean had been put in contact with us by Premier Peckford and we also knew Dean was fired by Doug Ford the previous year. We came to learn that Dean was as disturbed about the actions of the Ford government as the rest of us. There was nothing in it for Dean French, financially or otherwise, except to get some progress going and help us end the federal mandates. Only those who have no conceptual understanding of how negotiations or diplomacy works, would conclude that we were somehow conspiring with Dean French. We needed someone like him to get us access to the city, and then to the federal government. Dean didn't need us for anything!

We decided to take a break, and our host who brought Dean, ordered a bunch of pizzas, which was great for me because I was struggling to eat for most of my time in Ottawa and pizza is my favorite food. Dean left the room while the rest of us decided on a way forward, based on what the mayor was offering, and a final decision was made. At the conclusion of the meeting, we told Dean we were encouraged by what the mayor was saying but because the entire Board wasn't there, they would go away and meet with the rest, which is exactly what happened that night.

I didn't attend that meeting, because I was not a Board member, and I had no vote. However, from the POEC testimony, it was later revealed that the Board had unanimously agreed to move trucks out of the residential areas, in exchange for a meeting with the mayor.

The following morning, on the 12th, two letters were exchanged, with Board approval, between Tamara and the

Mayor. A "Letter from Mayor Watson to Tamara Lich requesting removal of trucks in return for meeting with Convoy" and a "Letter from Tamara Lich to Watson saying that Convoy Board agrees with the request to reduce pressure on residents and plans to consolidate efforts around Parliament Hill".

It wasn't made public that we had reached a deal with the Mayor, until the next day, the 13th. Unfortunately for us, word had not gotten out to the Convoy until later in the day when a group of us were going into a meeting at City Hall, to discuss the details of the move.

As we were walking into the building, Chris Barber's phone rang, and the conversation with the person who called was heated. At first, I didn't fully understand what was going on, but I quickly found out that a lot of the Truckers were very upset about the deal, because they were hearing about it through the media, and not through any of us.

As we were going into the meeting with Steve, the City Manager, Superintendent Robert Drummond, and Kim Ayotte, the man in charge of Emergency Preparedness, I noticed my phone was getting very low on battery, so I turned it off.

During this meeting, Chris Barber asked Steve why the city told all the businesses to shut down and told him we would have supported local shops. Chris went on to explain that he spoke to the closest Tim Horton's owner who said, "In two weeks, he had made as much as in the previous two years when business was down because of all the lockdowns."

After spending more time talking about specific areas of

concern for the city and that we would all try to relocate trucks, for the 3rd time, the meeting ended with agreement as per the terms of the letters between the Mayor and Tamara.

When the meeting ended, all hell broke loose when I turned on my phone. A now-former Board member who was close to Tamara had access to her Twitter account and at 8:24 p.m. sent a tweet in her name:

"More fake news. This time from CityTV News. No deal has been struck. The federal government has not yet lifted its mandates and passports. Do not watch #fakenews. It's bad for your mental health. This is completely false."

This tweet was an absolute disaster. One, for the fact that the federal government would later testify that they couldn't trust us because they accused us of reneging on the deal with Watson. Additionally, it confused many of the Truckers and they were getting demoralized. Even Randy Hillier sent out a tweet saying we had "sold out the Convoy" with this deal, although I can't actually confirm it was Randy who sent the tweet himself, and I later suspected he didn't.

During the POEC, we learned of a very interesting Ontario Provincial Police Officer named Inspector Marcel Beaudin, who was heavily involved with the Convoy from a Police Liaison Team perspective, or PLT. He testified that during the Convoy, on the 10th of February, he was contacted via email, by the Deputy Minister of Public Safety, Rob Stewart. After several email exchanges and various phone calls between the OPP, OPS, and the DM of Public Safety, there was an appetite to offer a meeting, between the Convoy leadership and potential Ministers. However, at that time, meetings would only be considered if we would agree to denounce all illegal activity and exit the city. To be clear, this situation never developed to the point where we were presented with this offer from government officials, by any level of police. Inspector Beaudin was also in email communication with the Commissioner of the RCMP, Brenda Lucki.

On the 11th of February, a draft proposal document called, "Trucker Protest Engagement" was being formulated between Stewart, Lucki, and Inspector Beaudin. The Objective of the engagement plan was to, "de-escalate and encourage people to leave unlawful protest". The stated principles of the engagement plan were, "coordinate effectively with police, based on their advice" and to, "listen and explain the government's position – NO negotiation".

The second principle was the government stating they would have no negotiation authority if they had agreed to meet with any of us. When asked if Inspector Beaudin felt the draft engagement plan would have been effective, he testified he believed it would have.

However, there were discussions among the police liaison teams. They guessed without any behavioral scientific evidence, that 60% of the Truckers would have left, had I announced we were leaving. They also believed that even if many of the Truckers left Ottawa, several would have remained and they would have had to deal with them, but it would have been a much smaller footprint.

I'm only speculating, but there was a belief that I controlled 322 vehicles in the downtown area. That number was because back on day four, I finally got a snapshot of what we had on that specific day. That number changed all the time, but what's interesting is that the police treated it like I had command of those vehicles, in reality, no one had any authority over individual Truckers!

There was a concern from law enforcement that they would be criticized for starting to arrest protesters and not give them an opportunity to leave, so one of the main efforts of the OPP, according to Inspector Beaudin, was to encourage as many protesters as possible to leave Ottawa before any type of enforcement activity began. To be fair, had I been in their shoes, I would have been looking at the same strategy, as a good policy of public safety while balancing the rights of citizens to peacefully assemble. There were members of the OPS, Deputy Chief Ferguson included, who were also of the same philosophy as Inspector Beaudin, in this goal.

During the POEC, our lawyer Brendan Miller cross-examined Inspector Beaudin about his engagement proposal. Brendan established that neither Rob Stewart Deputy Minister of Public Safety nor Commissioner Brenda Lucki of the RCMP, had issues with the proposal to engage identified leadership from the Convoy in deliberate dialogue, to get us to withdraw from the city and avoid enforcement action. But that plan was never approved by the political leadership of the federal government.

Brendan asked a follow-up question, "And in your

interactions with the Deputy Minister and Commissioner Lucki after February 12th, 2022, did they tell you anything about what happened with this proposal?" for which Inspector Beaudin replied, "I think the proposal was kind of, like, dead in the water after the 13th when the mayor provided his letter."

Brenden further asked Inspector Beaudin if he was aware that the engagement proposal was presented to Federal Cabinet Ministers at their *Incident Response Group* or IRG meeting at 3:30 p.m. on the afternoon of the 13th. Inspector Beaudin was not aware that his plan was briefed to Cabinet but the very next day the Prime Minister of Canada invoked The Emergencies Act, instead of listening to the advice of the Deputy Minister of Public Safety, the Commissioner of the RCMP and Inspector Beaudin of the OPP.

One of the things Inspector Beaudin commented on during his testimony was, as with every protest, the leadership of the protesters would eventually start infighting. In our case, it was also true, but I didn't see a lot of it during the Convoy. It wouldn't be until six months later that I would start to hear about all of it! The infighting went from being private to being fully publicized through social media. We had a few bad actors among us, and it cost us, and millions of Canadians dearly.

Chapter 13

No Deal

Tamara and the Mayor of Ottawa had exchanged letters on February 12th but the following day a news report came out in the mainstream media, CityNews, that no deal had been struck between us and the city.

That disastrous tweet of February 13th at 8:24 p.m. caused absolute chaos and unfortunately, the situation became even more controversial because that same trusted person, just three minutes later, retweeted the original post, making it look like Tamara retweeted at 8:27 p.m., "The media lies to their viewers, no "deal" has been made. End the mandates. End the passports. That's why we are here."

The person in question is someone I hardly had any exposure to, and I didn't see them as a significant member of the team. In July following the Convoy, I had to be reminded who this person was. I had no reason to spend much time with this person, but I regret that now because perhaps their activities could have been contained.

To this day, there is a lot of confusion as to why this person publicly denied that a deal had been struck, when in fact the entire Board, myself, Eva, and Keith, as well as this person, knew about the deal. I have my suspicions but in the grand scheme of things, it really doesn't matter. I think the government was always looking for any justification to invoke The Emergencies Act, and this person's actions gave them the justifications and cover they needed to do it, especially in the media.

It wasn't until the POEC that we all heard the testimony of the Prime Minister and his justifications for invoking The Emergencies Act. When Eva Chipiuk cross-examined Justin Trudeau during the POEC, she asked him, "On the Sunday night, February 13th, there was an IRG meeting, and you were there, and in fact, you were the Chair of that meeting; is that correct?" and he responded, "Yes." Eva continued her next question with, "And at the IRG meeting, you were advised that there were breakthrough -- there was a breakthrough agreement between the Mayor of Ottawa and the Convoy organizers to move trucks out of the downtown residential areas; isn't that correct?"

At this point, Trudeau was being a little cagey, about who he understood the agreement (between the Mayor and the Convoy) was with. Eva persisted and informed him that it was Tamara's name on the agreement between us and the Mayor. Eva continued further, "It was made publicly available on the news on Sunday, February 13th, and you were advised of that agreement at the IRG meeting."

Trudeau then replied, "And we were also advised that that agreement wasn't holding and that many of the Convoy had decried it as fake news and not actually an agreement that they would abide by."

Sitting in the audience, listening to Justin Trudeau admit that they discounted our commitment to the deal at the IRG meeting, because of two Twitter posts, was unbelievably frustrating, but only because one of our own people gave the Prime Minister the convenient excuse he needed to invoke The Emergencies Act.

I believe he was looking for a reason as early as the 27th of January 2022, but he was handed the perfect excuse to pull the trigger that night.

The next day, at 4:30 pm, Justin Trudeau publicly announced that he was invoking The Emergencies Act against his own citizens.

Ironically, on the exact same day, Justin Trudeau invoked The Emergencies Act, we finally succeeded in moving trucks in accordance with the original deal. With the help of the OPS and OPP, approximately twenty trucks were moved to Wellington, forty trucks left the downtown core, and about 100 cars and trucks moved from residential streets and completely cleared out two residential blocks.

Chapter 14

The Seinfeld of Intelligence Gathering: Using the MOU and Diagolon to Justify The Emergencies Act

Part 1

A few days before February 8th, 2022, I kept hearing rumblings about an MOU, or Memorandum of Understanding. With everything going on, I didn't have a lot of time to look into it. However, the MOU found time to deal with me!

I found out that the MOU had been sent to the Federal Government via Registered Mail, long before the Convoy arrived in Ottawa and that Canada Unity founders, James Bauder and Martin Broadman, had been working on this document for close to a year, if not longer.

I liked Martin. He was often in the meetings I was in, but I had no idea why he was there. This was the case with so many people. It was common for me not to know everyone who attended, but I always assumed they had been invited by someone.

I knew Martin always had good intentions, but I quickly learned he was working on a separate agenda from the rest of us. I can say the same thing about many of the other groups as well. The truth is, I didn't care all that much. Regardless of the organization you were with, I just acted as though everyone was on "Team Canada".

At some point on the 7th of February, I learned that Canada Unity had released the MOU to the public and the mainstream media was loving it, because it gave them a golden opportunity to act like this was a January 6th event, similar to what happened in Washington D.C., the previous year. We were very aware that the media and Government were looking for a way to make the Convoy their own "Canadian January 6th". We were always on the lookout for the potential for this to happen to us and the media outright lied about everything written in the MOU.

Parts of the MOU can be interpreted in many different ways. If you take the time to read the details, what you can't deny is that it calls for the Governor General and the Senate, to form a unified committee, as representatives of the highest levels of the federal government, and in that capacity, direct all other levels of government to:

"...immediately cease and desist all unconstitutional human rights, discriminatory and segregated actions, and not limited to, immediately instruct all levels of the federal, provincial, territorial and municipal governments to not only stop, but furthermore waive all SARS-CoV-2 (and not limited to SARS-CoV-2 10 subsequent variations) fines that have been issued and imposed upon its citizens, institutions, and private enterprises."

Furthermore:

"...instruct all levels of the federal, provincial, territorial, and municipal governments to re-instate all employees in all branches of governments [...] private industry and institutional sectors employees with full lawful employment rights prior to the wrongful and unlawful dismissals that stem from the SARS-CoV-2 and [...] subsequent [...]vaccine passport mandates."

However, there is one paragraph the media and government focused their attention on, only for the purpose of further fortifying their vilification of all of us:

"In this case the parties are, "THE PEOPLE OF CANADA", the "SENATE OF CANADA", and "THE GOVERNOR GENERAL OF CANADA", the highest authorities representing the federal government. The matter to be discussed and agreed upon is this; The Senate of Canada and the Governor General, combined referred to as the Federal Government are to uphold and enforce all Canadian and International Human Rights Laws

that are clearly laid out in the MOU or "RESIGN their lawful positions of authority Immediately".

The last part of the sentence was used to say, we were there to overthrow the government. Had the last section of the MOU not been written, with the word RESIGN, they wouldn't have had anything to credibly use against everyone.

What was never mentioned by the MSM was the line *"The matter to be discussed and agreed upon is this;"* The goal of the MOU was always to have a discussion with the government about either upholding the laws or asking them to resign if they refused to uphold them. Of note, this document generated a petition that over 300,000 Canadians agreed with and signed.

There are three critical points that need to be considered. First, the MOU holds no force and effect and is only meant to seek that two parties agree to hold discussions at a future time. Had the Governor General and Senate signed this MOU, it would have only set the terms for having a future discussion with a newly formed group called the Citizens of Canada Committee, within ninety days of signing.

Second, nowhere in the MOU does it say that the intent is to abolish the current Liberal Government of Canada from being the elected government. In fact, the goal is for the Governor General and Senate to work with direct representatives of the People, as the Citizens of Canada Committee, and direct all levels of government to stop all Covid-19 related mandates.

Third, nowhere does the MOU call for an overthrow of the government. There is no mention of violence and there is no "Or

Else!" threat in the entire document.

Additionally, the original MOU was sent to all federal political parties, the Senate, and the Governor General – by registered mail! To my knowledge, even if the MOU had requested the Governor General to dissolve the government, or for her to resign, that in itself, is not an illegal request. It's also not exactly a method one would choose to threaten to overthrow anyone as it lacks a sufficient amount of fear or serious threat of violence!

But that's not how the Liberal Government, the NDP, and most of the media spun it. They lied about the Convoy deliberately trying to overthrow the elected government and that the Convoy was an insurrection led by right-wing extremists, Nazis, and misogynists. They kept repeating that same lie over and over until many Canadians believed it was true.

Months later I agreed to go on a podcast with a very contentious former shock-jock, who claimed we tried to overthrow the government but refused to even let me explain the issues with the MOU during the podcast. The truth was irrelevant to him and his audience. Even a year later, the leader of the NDP was spouting off the same lies that had already been disproven during the POEC. The testimony under oath is all over the internet, and we still have politicians and media telling the same lies about the MOU.

Unfortunately, I took on the unenviable task of requesting that Martin Broadman retract the MOU. No one asked me to talk to him. I just knew I had to, and I wanted to be as respectful as possible. I was incredibly conflicted about having this conversation, but we were getting killed in the media, and by many of our supporters. I had seen a document that appeared to be somewhat contentious, and I thought I was reading the actual MOU. It wasn't until I was on the stand at the POEC, that I saw the original MOU. To this day, I'm not sure what it was I read during the Convoy.

In the conversation with Martin, I learned that he had been working on this document for months. I didn't want to disrespect their efforts, but it was sending a very confusing message to everyone. It was also something that wasn't sanctioned by the rest of the Convoy, Freedom Corp., and any other group. I knew Police on Guard were very upset about this too. Their name was being associated with potentially overthrowing the government and they were not impressed at all, because it wasn't true.

I recall the conversation getting very strained, but I finally told Martin that if Canada Unity didn't rescind the MOU, Freedom Corp. would have no choice but to denounce it. It was a very hard moment for both of us because I knew what they had done to finally have the attention of the Government of Canada, but it was exactly the wrong kind of attention focused on us.

Reluctantly, and to Martin's credit, he agreed to rescind the MOU because he recognized the damage that had been done to all of us. I certainly don't want to take any credit for causing the MOU to be rescinded, because I'm sure the message to Martin and James was universal by many groups, but on the 8th of February, Canada Unity publicly rescinded the MOU.

To make matters worse, that's the exact same day I had misspoken publicly on a live stream, about "forming a coalition government" and working together to stop the Liberal mandates. As unfortunate as the timing was, I had no knowledge of the contents of the actual MOU when I uttered those words.

Even with the MOU retraction, and my public clarification on the 10th of February, the toothpaste was already out of the tube, and the media and government were going to use it as part of their justification to invoke The Emergencies Act, which they did.

Part 2

About six months before the Convoy, I was talking to my friend Braven, who is unusually gifted in politics, economics, and pop culture. He told me about an internet meme about a fictitious group called Diagolon.

Now, fast-forward to the Convoy, where I heard about a combat veteran, Jeremy MacKenzie from Nova Scotia, who was in Ottawa. At the time, I had no idea he was the creator of Diagolon. I had seen a lot of videos from his Instagram account, and although it was political satire, it was reminiscent of George Carlin's style of humor. It was always hilarious because you realized George was telling you the truth about the state of the world. Jeremy's humor is just as powerful.

I asked Dana Metcalf, if she had Jeremy's contact info, and thankfully she did. I had a quick phone conversation with him about army stuff and people we both knew from CFB Petawawa and Gagetown. After a few laughs, we agreed to stay in touch.

Somewhere around February 11th, multiple people sent me a video of a woman named The Amazing Polly. I had seen some of her content before because she had been outspoken, but heavily censored. The video was about a letter that was put out by the Convoy Board explaining that there were only four official spokespeople for the Convoy. During the video, she showed a clip of Jeremy MacKenzie, calling out two people, who were on that list authorized by the Board to speak.

As I watched the video, all I could think of is how this video couldn't have come at a worse time. I couldn't care less about the content of the message, but I definitely cared about the timing of it. I felt it could have been dealt with either privately, or after the Convoy ended. Sometimes, people who think they have important information to share, don't want to hold off in case someone else breaks the story first.

I can tell you, it was something I had to deal with for nearly four full days. Instead of looking after Convoy issues, I was completely taken off task, dealing with this nonsense. My good friend Serena called me to talk about it and vouched for Polly and said her work was always very good and credible. My response was that I didn't care what the content was about because now instead of dealing with how to get a dialogue going with the politicians, I was having to deal with this nothing burger.

This wasn't going away, and I now had to grapple with supporters of both Polly and Jeremy. In the end, what they said in their video, was very valid, but the timing was absolutely terrible and unnecessary.

I should have paid closer attention to what Jeremy and Polly said in that video, because to this very day, the former Board member they called out, has been harassing me, Keith, Eva, and Jeremy all over social media. Months later, in July of 2022, Keith sent me a link to a podcast where the same person they talked about – the one responsible for sending the disastrous tweet that nullified our deal, was insinuating I sabotaged the Convoy. These attacks have continued ever since!

No, I will not use his name here, nor anywhere else in this book but I will say this person turned out to be very harmful to the entire Convoy, during and after.

When The Emergencies Act was declared, the federal government was required to hold debates and to ratify the decision, in both the House of Commons and the Senate, within seven days. A vote must be passed in the House and then it must go to the Senate. During the debate in the House, the Liberal Party and the NDP kept referencing the group known as Diagolon.

Well, that's when people started sending me videos again, but this time they were of Jeremy and some of his close friends at the Convoy. They created a video showing the MPs, one after another, mentioning Diagolon as justification for invoking The Emergencies Act.

It was absolutely ridiculous. I called Jeremy and asked him to tell me everything there was to know about Diagolon. He explained to me that it was a joke he started because he noticed that all of the US States and Canadian Provinces that did not have mask mandates, formed a diagonal line from Alaska through Alberta to Texas. Those that had mask mandates, form a circle around those that don't, which is where Circulon, the arch-enemy of Diagolon, came from.

Jeremy said he made the Diagolon symbol, sitting on the toilet with his iPhone, in about three seconds, and that the joke started as a means of getting strangers to rally around something funny and come to a BBQ for comradery.

The reason I'm writing about the MOU and Diagolon is because, during my testimony at the POEC, I was cross-examined about both of these issues.

When asked about Diagolon during my testimony and the video that Jeremy and his friends had done while watching the House of Commons debate, I commented, "And yet here he was, watching members of Parliament and the Liberal Party seriously stating that the reason for invoking The Emergencies Act was because of Diagolon. It was the most outrageous ridiculous thing I had ever seen. And I think this Commission should be investigating that, as the biggest Intelligence joke of the last decade. So it's a joke. Diagolon is a joke. It's not even a real thing."

Even as of this writing, every Google search will say that Diagolon is an ultra-right-wing extremist militia. What they don't say is that the Vice President of Diagolon, Vice President Philip, is actually a plastic, time-traveling, cocaine-addicted goat figurine, that sits on Jeremy's desk during his podcasts.

The Liberal Government of Canada, with the support of the NDP, hung their justification for invoking The Emergencies Act on the MOU and Diagolon.

Chapter 15

The Emergencies Act and a Lesson from Premier Brian Peckford

I was having a conversation with Keith and Eva about the possibility of negotiations with the government going forward, which we hoped would eventually happen. I intended that if we got into a good negotiation with the government, we could bring former Premier Brian Peckford in as the closer.

In that conversation, I very cautiously asked them if I would be able to meet Mr. Peckford for a quick conversation. I wanted to ask what he was thinking, about how we could progress things between one of the levels of government to get things going. I said cautiously because I didn't want anyone to get the impression that I was inappropriately asking to meet with him. It was genuinely to understand his perspective and to have a really good conversation that we could build from. What I didn't want was a large room full of people. I was hoping for just me and Keith and Eva and maybe Tamara or Chris and Mr. Peckford. The smaller the group the better, because there are many distractions when a room is too full of people with varying degrees of questions and comments. I was happy Keith set it up for the next morning, February 14th.

He gave me the time, the place was the Lord Elgin Hotel, and we had a room on the top floor that was used for conferences. When I arrived for the meeting, there were several people just finishing up with Mr. Peckford, so I waited patiently. Eva had already arrived and as everyone else left, I exchanged the typical pleasantries with Mr. Peckford and his wife Carol. As we sat down for a coffee it struck me as totally surreal, because there I was sitting with Premier Brian Peckford, whom just a few weeks before, I was watching on Jordan Peterson's podcast, and now I was having a coffee with him.

It was incredible for me. He gave me a lot of background information on the Charter of Rights and Freedoms in Canada and what his involvement was. It was like sitting down and having a coffee with one of the American founding fathers, to discuss the American constitution.

In that conversation, we discussed the state of Canada and knew we were all in Ottawa because we were very concerned. At some point, Keith Wilson walked into the room and apologized to everybody for interrupting, and said, "Mr. Premier I need to inform you that the Prime Minister has just invoked The Emergencies Act."

Keith said he remembered Premier Peckford's response very differently from my memory of it, but I'm going to defer to Keith on this because my memory of events, likely colored by my feelings, included some foul language from Premier Peckford, which I'll leave out!

In Keith's version, Premier Peckford folded his hands together, looked down, and said, "Oh Lord." My version was considerably less dignified.

Keith was accompanied by Tamara. She quickly joined the rest of us at the table and we started to formulate some form of response. At one point I asked Mr. Peckford if he would be willing to participate in a joint statement with Tamara and he agreed without hesitation. Initially, I wanted him to come in for the final phases of any negotiation but given that the situation had fundamentally changed with the invocation of The Emergencies Act, I felt we needed to have the biggest gun in our arsenal to shoot back. What could be better than sending in one of the original signatures of the Charter of Rights and Freedoms of Canada?

That's when we saw people really mobilize and start drafting Tamara's statement, which she would give that afternoon at the

Westin Hotel, accompanied by Premier Peckford.

This was one of those rare occasions when we invited mainstream media. Everyone was given time to set up for the press conference. The room was packed with supporters, mainstream media, and citizen journalists. Unfortunately, one of the worst of the worst, a GlobalTV journalist showed up. After the statements from both Tamara and Mr. Peckford, this GlobalTV buffoon shouted out the first folly of questions. He became so aggressive with his questioning that I approached him and said if he continued, I would have security remove him from the building. It didn't matter anyway because we shut the press conference down almost immediately after that. Again, another missed opportunity for mainstream media journalists to do real journalism. They had a man with Brian Peckford's legacy available to them to answer meaningful questions about the suspension of the Charter of Rights and Freedoms. Yet, they couldn't muster the professionalism to ask simple questions. And they wonder why the public no longer trusts them and treats their profession with such contempt.

Chapter 16

Roadmap to Freedom and Missed Opportunities

It was late afternoon, after The Emergencies Act had been invoked, and I was sitting on a bench in one of the hallways of the Arc Hotel near the elevator with Keith and Eva. Nobody was down that hallway, so we seemed to have it all to ourselves. For some reason I remember that I was on a bench, Eva was sitting beside me, and Keith was kneeling in front of us on the floor. We were strategizing on how we could get the ball rolling because of The Emergencies Act. I remember saying to Keith, "One of the reasons I'm here is because I think we need a public inquiry into everything the government has done related to the handling of Covid-19." I said, "I'm old enough to remember the Somalia inquiry that was televised for several weeks. The public got to see what had transpired in that inquiry which ultimately led to the Liberal government of the time completely disbanding the Airborne Regiment for various reasons." When I mentioned the public inquiry, Keith looked at me as his mind started to work out some complicated legal calculous. Keith mentioned he was one of a very small handful of lawyers that he knew, who had been involved in a public inquiry previously, so he'd been through this once before in his career. Ideas started to form around a document about what we should do next.

I'm not talking about an MOU or anything like that. What we wanted to do was give the public a very clear understanding of why we were all in Ottawa protesting. Keith, Tamara, and others started to create a document we called, "The Roadmap to Freedom."

"We began our Freedom Convoy with a clear destination. Restoring freedom for our families, our neighbors, and our country. We rolled into Ottawa nineteen days ago taking a stand for our future.

We have given hope and power to freedom-loving Canadians and beyond. People from around the world are now standing with us and want their freedoms back.

Our message to all government has been clear from the start - we want our freedoms restored. To say the least, our government's reactions to Covid and the restrictions imposed on our lives, kids, and businesses over the last two years have been very difficult for everyone. Families have been separated, kids have lost education and social development, people have been censored, bullied, and shamed, and people have lost their jobs and livelihoods. We have lost our fundamental rights and freedoms. Worst of all, so many Canadians have lost hope.

We are calling on all governments in Canada to restore the rights and freedoms of Canadians and set concrete limits so governments can't easily abuse our rights and limit our freedoms again.

It is now time for serious and immediate action by our governments.

We call upon our governments to restore the rights and freedoms of all Canadians:

1. End all vaccine mandates for all Canadians, Truckers, travelers, employees, health-care workers, law enforcement agents, and soldiers;

2. Cancel provincial and municipal vaccine passports and masking requirements;

3. End all state-of-emergency declarations;

4. Allow those who have lost their jobs to go back to work;

5. Grant access to parents that lost access to their kids - be reunited;

6. Financial protection for the small businesses

harmed by Covid restrictions; and

7. Respect freedom of choice and not discriminate.

We call upon our governments to ensure we don't make this mistake again:

1. Supreme Court of Canada Review of Government Actions

We need to know whether our rights under the Charter mean anything. We call upon the Federal Government to initiate a Constitutional Reference question to the Supreme Court of Canada about the constitutional validity of the Covid laws and restrictions.

2. Public Inquiry of Government's Response to Covid

As a matter of national importance, we call upon the Federal Government to appoint a fully independent and impartial public inquiry on the government's handling of Covid responses.

We need to know what went wrong—what caused governments to so easily trample our rights and freedoms and cause so much harm to our people and our nation.

For the inquiry to be effective, the following conditions must be considered:

a) The inquiry members to be selected by an all-party parliamentary process;

b) It must contain a thorough examination of the

science, policy responses and the consequences;

c) It must be commenced by March 20, 2022; and

d) It must be public and live-streamed.

It is time to heal the divisions that have been created in our families, in our communities, and our Country.

This has gone on far too long. We are calling upon all levels of government to do the right thing for our families, communities, and Canada.

The Freedom Convoy 2022

One of the things we were asking for, was a public inquiry into the steps that led to COVID-19 lockdowns and mandates. But we wanted input about that, so we were in consultation with Premier Brian Peckford as he also had experience in this area. The irony is that invoking The Emergencies Act itself, under Section 63 of the Act, meant that as soon as Trudeau did so, he had to have a public inquiry.

While writing this book, there has been a National Citizen's Inquiry, which is a citizen-led and citizen-funded initiative to hear testimony of how Covid-19 affected people's lives all across Canada, as well as the Public Order Emergency Commission required by invoking the Act.

Other activities were happening at that time. It was a very hectic week after the events of February 14th. Keith and Eva were extremely busy writing this new document. Part of the goal was really to reinforce a clear understanding to various levels of government, and to all of our supporters as well as our detractors, what we were there for.

In hindsight, it is a document that we should have written as soon as the three of us started working together in Ottawa. Our social media campaign messages were very contradictory, and we didn't have a cohesive or coordinated plan with one specific spokesperson. Although attempts were made, the media messaging just wasn't consistent. It was an absolute free-for-all as we didn’t have an overall organized strategic plan on how we wanted to communicate to the public. In hindsight, given my three priorities, social media messaging should have been something I was much more involved in.

When I read the first draft of The Roadmap to Freedom document, I thought it was brilliant. The decision was made for Tamara to read it on a live-stream. As I've said before, watching Tamara give a speech at a podium, or do a live stream, is like watching somebody who has done this professionally for decades.

The background to this story is that there was another press conference during the day with Tamara and Premier Peckford. The consensus, within the Convoy leadership, was that they wanted to focus on what they were doing with Premier Peckford. But in my estimation, there was a serious timing issue.

Even though I was the one who asked Premier Peckford if he would be willing to do a public statement, right after we learned about The Emergencies Act, I didn't think we should be doing the press conference with him at that point. I regret that I wasn't more assertive in my discussions with Tamara, Keith, Eva, and some of the others. I had a discussion with Keith where I believed that The Road Map to Freedom document, should be the priority and he said to me “I'm not seeing this the way you're seeing it, walk me through it”.

I said something to the effect of, “We're heading into the weekend and the House of Commons has already voted in favor of The Emergencies Act, but it hasn't gone to the Senate yet. What we need to do is give the Conservative Party some sort of a life raft. Something they can look at as being a very reasonable request on our part and then go into Parliament to advocate on our behalf.”

Now, I know initially, I wasn't getting through, but in the conversation with Keith, we were looking at the news cycle, the time of day, and the fact that we were going into the weekend. My ultimate aim for that document was for the Conservatives to grab hold of it and try to get some sort of last-minute emergency debate going in the House of Commons. Potentially that debate could have had an influence on the Senate because we understood the Senate would then have to vote in favor in order to continue with The Emergencies Act.

I was struggling to communicate what I was thinking effectively, and one of the reasons it was difficult was because I knew it was an absolute last resort with very little chance of success, and I wasn't convinced the Conservatives were even going to take notice of our activity.

One of the things that is truly impressive about Keith Wilson is that he plays three-dimensional chess in his head. He'd often say to me, “Okay, what do you see? Let's game it out.” This was great for me, as it allowed me to grow an idea in a manner that helps me think tactically about specific situations. This also allowed Keith and I to work very well together in that regard.

As I talked to Keith, I tried to explain the timing and the effect it may or may not have on the Conservative Party, all the while acknowledging I might just be very naive, which was more likely the case. At the time, the coalition government between the Federal Liberals and the New Democratic Party hadn't been made public yet, so we hoped the Conservatives would grab onto this idea, as something reasonable and measured that they could get behind and put political pressure on the Trudeau government.

The document was finally ready. We had somebody we were working with on media strategy and social media. Some conflicting things had been spread around about this person publicly, but that was totally irrelevant to me at the time, so I disregarded it and just focused on the tasks at hand.

This person was also involved in organizing the live-stream, where Tamara would be delivering The Road Map to Freedom document. Before Tamara began, I specifically asked this person, if as planned, The Road Map to Freedom document was going to be sent to every single Federal Member of Parliament via email and I was assured, at that moment, that all their email addresses were loaded into the laptop. All we had to do was hit the send button, and every MP would get a copy of The Road Map to Freedom document, the moment Tamara started speaking.

Regrettably, I made the monumental mistake of not confirming that the document was sent as planned, until the next morning. I sent a text message to the person who assured me the document was going to be emailed the night before and the response I got was, “No, we're doing some polishing on the document.”

At this point I wasn't sure who I was angrier with; the person I had relied on to send out the document, or myself for not confirming that the document was actually sent at the agreed time.

I've had time to reflect on this but ultimately it was my carelessness that let it happen. I remember receiving that text response and immediately getting on the phone with Keith and Eva. Unfortunately, once again I let my frustration get the better of me and I was screaming at Keith and Eva on the phone, but my anger wasn’t towards either of them. I was angry about what happened and was venting because my concern was that Tamara had given a live public statement the night before and we were going to put out a different document that didn’t match word-for-word what Tamara had stated publicly. Because they wouldn’t be exactly the same, I knew the media, or some other entity, would pick apart the differences. Second to that, it was yet one more delay and I had wanted this statement made at least twenty-four hours previous to when it was released because of the Conservative Party needing time to act on the document if they could.

One of the reasons I was given as to why the document didn't go out to the Members of Parliament when planned, was because the person responsible, or at least who committed to doing the task of sending it, told me that she had a headache and was tired.

While I am sympathetic to the discomforts of the human body, throughout most of the Convoy, I believe I had COVID-19. There are moments when you must push past physical discomfort and to me, this certainly qualified as one of those moments.

To be perfectly honest, except the one copy I personally sent to Pierre Poilievre through his public e-mail, I can't be sure if the document ever actually was emailed to any federal Member of Parliament. Also, to this day I never received acknowledgement of any kind that his staff or he had seen it.

Because of what happened, as a backup, on two separate occasions, I read portions of The Road Map to Freedom document publicly. I read it on a live-stream the evening of February 17th, and then again at the Lord Elgin Hotel at the press conference that Danny Bulford and I did together. One of the factors that made this so important, was the fiasco with the MOU that was submitted via registered mail to the Governor General of Canada and the Senate.

The Road Map to Freedom was a well thought out document and it hit on all the key points that represented the grievances that so many Canadians were feeling in the previous two years before the Convoy. For me, what was vitally important was the public inquiry, which in the end you can say that I did get, but it was through no effort of my own because it was already mandated. Regardless of how it happened, an inquiry still did go forward, even though it was a complete sham.

Reflecting on how important that document truly was, I think the shortcomings surrounding it were threefold:

First, it should have been something we produced within the

first week of being in Ottawa, so that the media, the public, and the government had a clear understanding of why we were there.

Second, I'm not one for making excuses but I would definitely chalk that up to learning tough lessons in the fog of war.

Third, it was my responsibility to make sure the Roadmap to Freedom e-mail was loaded even before Tamara started speaking on the livestream and there was no excuse for why I failed to follow up on the email delivery. I should never have left it in someone else's hands.

I had the experience from the military, of knowing that when your main effort is being executed, following up is of paramount importance, so you don't have a single source of failure.

It was unreasonable to leave it to chance, that the interim leader of the Conservative Party or any other member of the federal government, would have seen Tamara's live stream and pass the information up through their own chain of command. When it is that crucially important to your mission, you have a duty and a responsibility to ensure that you get confirmation that action was taken. This may seem like micromanagement, but when the detail is that important, there's no excuse for you not to confirm the agreed-upon course of action by people on your team.

If I could go back in time, I certainly would have ensured this document, or a clear statement from the Convoy, was given to the media and the government, within the first three days of my arrival. I also would have guaranteed that the document would have gone to the only people in Ottawa who could have done something about the requests made in The Road Map to Freedom.

These are the two major failures that could have better positioned all stakeholders to get to the peaceful resolution that we were looking for. I believe in my heart that The Road Map to Freedom document Keith wrote would have made a major difference in the outcome of the Convoy. I make that statement with the benefit of hindsight and ironically, after hearing the testimony of the POEC and knowing the results of the Commission's findings.

Chapter 17

Day of Days

Each weekend during the Convoy, there was a massive influx of Canadians from all around Quebec, Ontario, and other locations, that would flood into the downtown core of Ottawa to participate in and support the protest. Sometimes I thought of it as Canada Day One, Canada Day Two, Canada Day Three, and so on. Unfortunately, the weekend of Canada Day Four was coming up and on the previous Monday, February 14th, Justin Trudeau invoked The Emergencies Act.

This was the time I started paying very close attention to the weather because I knew it could potentially have an impact on where and when the police took action against us now that The Emergencies Act had been invoked.

On the Monday following invocation of The Emergencies Act, it was -15C/5F. On Tuesday I was hoping we were going to get a major weather event. My objective was just to make it to the following Monday, and the reason for this was that I was still very eager for the Conservative Party of Canada to do some political maneuvering of some kind and put an end to Justin Trudeau's invocation of The Emergencies Act. While I fully acknowledge this was naive thinking, we were running out of options to get any resemblance of a negotiation with the Trudeau government.

I noticed on the next day, Tuesday, that it was getting warmer outside, and this was causing me great concern because I knew that if the weather was favorable to them, the police would be more inclined to take action.

I believe it was either Monday or Tuesday that I received a phone call from an OPP Officer. I don't remember his name, but I certainly remember the impact he had on me. I learned very early in my military career to never get intimidated by another human being. But there was something very unusual about this particular OPP officer. I don't want to say I was intimidated or afraid, but whoever this man was, he was very professional and from what I gathered he was very experienced in these types of situations.

During the conversation, he explained that when there's a very difficult and prolonged situation between the government and a body of protesters, he's the guy they bring in. In my mind, I had this impression it was the Mr. Wolf character from the Pulp Fiction movie, but he certainly didn't act or sound like Harvey Keitel. This officer was straight to the point. His words were very well chosen and from what I could tell, selected based on a lot of behavioral science. Once we reviewed his resume, the introductory remarks did venture into a little bit of flattery as an attempt to stroke my ego. However, I was completely unaffected by it, because I understood it was part of this specific form of dialogue which was appropriate given the situation. During my MBA, an area I focused on with my electives was negotiations, and I've taken further negotiation training subsequent to my MBA. I understood the structure and vocabulary being used in this particular conversation.

One thing that was perfectly clear to me, was that I had met my match. This officer effortlessly achieved the desired impact. He got into my head in terms of conveying the seriousness of the situation, and he did it in a very non-threatening and non-aggressive way. I was quite impressed with the level of skill he brought to the conversation because he conveyed a lot of subtext with very few words.

The most important thing I took away from that phone call was a sense of timing. While he didn't specifically say which day the police were going to start making arrests, I could see it was inevitable that it would start happening just before the weekend, when all the Canadians who had been supporting the Convoy were routinely coming into the city. It was obvious to us, and law enforcement, that Canada Day Four was going to be the most critical weekend.

And this was why the weather became so important to me. By Wednesday the 16th the weather had gone into the plus temperature range with a high of 6C/43F. My concern was that we weren't going to make it to Canada Day Four and that if the weather started to turn much warmer the police would take action sooner. If it were possible for me to have manipulated the weather, to make it cold and very snowy, I certainly would have done that. By the 17th, the weather was still 6C/43F, but it had started to rain, so I was looking at the weather almost hourly and praying for a snowstorm. Again, my goal was to get to Monday to buy time for the Conservatives, so we had to get through the weekend.

The prayers worked and we actually did get a snowstorm starting in the middle of the evening of the 17th. That snowstorm was exactly what I was hoping for because I believed it would make it much more difficult for the police to come in and start kettling the protestors and making mass arrests. It also would have been more difficult for them to get some of their heavier paramilitary vehicles into the downtown core up on Wellington. As well, it would be difficult for them to get heavy equipment and start towing trucks or removing concrete barriers.

Unfortunately, I did not account for the fact that, throughout the entire Convoy, the truck drivers themselves had been shoveling the sidewalks and the roads all around each and every one of their vehicles. The irony was that their desire to be good stewards of the area, rendered the snowstorm completely useless, allowing the police to have the mobility they needed for mass arrests. I didn't notice until late Thursday evening, when I went out to assess the impact of the snow on the police effort, that the Truckers had removed it all themselves. All of my wishing, praying, and hoping for bad weather, was completely neutralized because we cleared the snow ourselves!

The next morning on February 18th, which was the Friday leading into Canada Day Four, the police commenced mass arrests using their Public Order Units from several different police departments across Canada.

In the late morning, I had gone to the intersection of Rideau and Sussex, to see for myself what was happening. I walked up to the line very close to where the protesters were facing off with a wall of Quebec Provincial Police officers, and to the South of them was a large group of OPP. On the rooftop of the Senate building, you could see sniper teams and overhead were also UAVs.

I distinctly remember approaching a large group of OPP officers and I could tell that my emotions were getting caught up in the moment. I had riot training through the military during Y2K, so I understood the concept of mob mentality. As I started getting closer to the group of police officers, I was looking at them and started clapping and in a very sarcastic manor, I thanked them for stealing my children's future, as well as the future of their children, by doing what they were doing. I will never forget how the vast majority of these police officers turned and looked back at me. What I saw was a group of officers, who if they could have shot me dead right there and then, like a dog in the street, without consequences, they would have done so.

I debated whether I'd mention that moment in this book because of my personal experiences working with police officers, on different occasions during my career in the Canadian Army. I also have many friends who are police officers in the province of Ontario. It's the job of a Public Order Unit to do crowd control and deal with riots. But I think it's an important moment to reflect on because it's vital to understand that it's not just protesters that are susceptible to mob mentality. The police are susceptible as well, but it is generally mitigated by the tactics and training they receive as members of a POU. And I still believe, that within that group of police officers, at least some of them understood we were there on their behalf too, even while they were being our oppressors.

I heard of a few occasions where some protesters were face-to-face with police officers. They read the facial expressions of the officers and could see regret in their eyes. I was told that in rare instances police officers did engage in dialogue with the protesters on the front line, but they were immediately swapped out by their sergeants with those who would not talk to us.

There was a group of police officers inside the Chateau Laurier who were part of a chat group that used their personal cell phones to laugh and joke about beating up protesters, telling other officers to, "save some of the protesters" for them. They wanted their turn to go in and put the "jackboots" to the protesters. The important thing to note about that was, it was a police officer who took screen captures of the improper behavior among the police and shared it publicly for everybody to see.

After my one-sided interaction with the group of OPP officers on the south side of the street, I backed away and saw Lincoln Jay from Rebel News standing on top of one of the concrete barriers. I had a very quick chat with him, then Alexa Lavoie, also from Rebel, came to talk to me. I asked her who the police in the brown uniforms were because I believed they were Quebec Provincial Police. I had personally gone up to the line, to look at the uniforms and the only image on the shoulders of those in brown uniforms was a fleur-de-lis on the badge. Alexa had also confirmed with me that they were, in fact, Quebec Provincial Police called Sûreté du Québec.

Soon after, I approached the front line between the protesters and the police. I could hear a large commotion off to my left and this was when I first saw the Toronto Police Mounted Unit coming up the north flank of the police. On horseback, they quickly turned to the south and pushed their way between the front line of protesters and the front line of police.

From a tactical perspective, I thought what they did was brilliant. The horses forced the protesters to step back and separate from the police. As the horses passed, the police would step forward and occupy the ground that the protesters had just given up to the horses. These horses were Clydesdales and they were absolutely massive.

While I was impressed with the tactic itself, I was also forced to step back. Staying put would be like trying to stop a snowplow coming through. It was impossible.

There was some time between the first pass of the horses and when they came around again. Unfortunately, on the second pass, two of the protesters were caught up. They could not back up and were physically injured by the horses. One of the victims was an elderly indigenous woman named Candace. She was standing with a walker, which was why she couldn't move fast enough.

The rumors started by the media, and perpetuated by the Ottawa Police Acting Chief was that a protester threw a bicycle at one of the horses. I can confirm, from what I witnessed with my own eyes, that this was not true, and the Police UAVs could have confirmed it. I was fifteen feet away from Candace and the other man, who were run down by the horses. Fortunately, we had protesters who were medically trained and acting as paramedics, and they quickly responded to both of our people. I know Candace was taken to the hospital and treated for injuries to her shoulder. To this day I never learned what happened to the man who was also trampled by the horses.

Soon after, I was standing several rows back from the frontline and I saw a big Canadian Army veteran from the Van Doos in Quebec City. He was wearing his beret, his medals, and his Special Forces tab, as was common for many of the veterans who were in Ottawa throughout the entire protest.

I could feel my aggression start to push the adrenaline around my body and remember looking at this veteran and asking him if he would be willing to go in and start fighting. Thankfully - he immediately declined! In that moment I realized I was starting to succumb to a form of mob mentality, and it scared the hell out of me. I knew it was happening, while simultaneously knowing it was wrong, as we could not physically engage in violent activity with the police.

As a child, I grew up in some very rough neighborhoods, and

getting into fistfights was a regular occurrence. My father put me in martial arts when I was seven years old, and I've done years of military service having a certain mentality towards violence. I have to admit I don't like to fight, but I am very accustomed to and comfortable in situations where I may have to get physical with another person.

When I realized what was happening to me, I knew the best thing I could do for everybody was to vacate the area. So, I decided to walk down Wellington to see what was happening further to the west.

Shortly after my departure from the front line, where the protesters and police were, Alexa Lavoie, wearing full media credentials and carrying a microphone, was shot point blank in the thigh with a projectile. The police were now actively shooting at members of the media, but only the media that the Government of Canada did not like.

Because of The Emergencies Act and with the police now subsequently making their mass arrests, many of the supporters decided to start leaving after the morning of Friday, February 18th. Chris Barber had already been arrested on the 16th and it was the following evening, the 17th, that Tamara Lich was arrested. There was nobody left from within my circle of influence who I believed the public would recognize - someone who could give a public statement - except for me, Danny Bulford, and Keith. Perhaps Keith and I could have done a joint statement, but at that point, he was fully engaged with other issues, so Danny and I did a live stream from the Lord Elgin

Hotel.

This part was a blur to me, but at the end of our statement, I remember Danny making a direct, emotional appeal to the police, to stop what they were doing. He said something to the effect of, "I can tell you that I care more about you than your own chain of command does."

Immediately after we did that live stream, Danny was told there was a warrant for his arrest. I had been speaking to Constable Andrew Wierzbicki daily, so once Chris and Tamara were arrested, I kept asking the OPP if there was also a warrant for my arrest. The answer was always no. After leaving our live stream, Danny went directly to where the protest was facing off with the police. He approached an officer saying, "I hear there's a warrant for my arrest." and basically surrendered himself. What was concerning was the police officer did not bother to confirm if there was in fact, an actual warrant. Instead, he chose to make the arrest on Danny's word alone. As Danny described it later: It was only after he was processed and in a jail cell adjacent to Chris Barber, that it became known to the detective in charge that Danny was in custody. That detective became extremely annoyed when he realized there was no warrant, and that Danny should not have been in there.

As a result, Danny was released without charges and I'm not sure if there was ever an actual apology.

At some point that day, I got a text from my cousin Jay informing me that my uncle and grandfather were not too pleased with me. I think they were more concerned about the possibility of having their bank accounts frozen, than they were about me. I didn't take it too personally. We have the same last name and if their accounts got frozen, well, so be it. Welcome to the club of six million Canadians who actually had the courage to fight back. I joked with a friend that I was going to drop those family members' names and addresses in a live stream, and thank them as my biggest supporters, but I decided that wasn't going to be a very fun topic of discussion if I ever saw them again.

For me, it was yet another blatant example of how the most hated body of politicians in my lifetime, had so much power and influence in pitting family against family.

On the morning of the 19th of February, I had a meeting with several of the block captains, Decks, and a few others. We realized there was no value in remaining in Ottawa. We couldn't stop the Police, who had proven themselves to be more than willing to be violent.

As a group, we decided the best option was to recommend that the Truckers go home. From our perspective, we didn't get the mandates lifted, but getting Trudeau to show his true colors was a victory in itself.

We ended the meeting, and I decided I would notify the OPP by calling Constable Andrew Wierzbicki to tell him we would peacefully withdraw from Ottawa, but he needed to remove the concrete barriers and let us get fuel to leave. Leanne decided to grab her cell phone and record my conversation with Constable Wierzbicki.

Moments before I had made that call, I was watching the news and saw the images of the POU arresting people. The media was getting off on it and I was furious. As I was on the phone with him, I used a lot of profanity and mentioned that we were not going to just stay there and be their punching bags.

That afternoon, I also held another live stream press conference at 1 p.m., at the Lord Elgin Hotel and told everyone who showed up with a camera we were recommending that each trucker peacefully withdraw. I was very specific about my language.

Beginning that press conference was an incredibly difficult and emotional moment for me. I was very angry that the government used the police to brutalize us, and I was angry the police agreed to do it, especially given that to this day, the Convoy was never actually declared illegal. In fact, the opposite is true. When you hear government officials refer to the Convoy as “illegal”, they’re lying. It was never deemed illegal at any time and that has not changed to this day.

When I opened up the floor to questions, some disgusting media troll, who was sitting beside Andrew Lawton of True North Media, asked me questions about accountability for what we had done. I asked him, “What laws have we broken?” and he had no answer at all. He sat there tweeting viciously about what I was saying. I answered the question for him which was that we broke some by-laws regarding parking infractions.

Over his shoulder were two of the most courageous people I’ve ever met, Roy and Nicole, the former owners of Peterburgers restaurant in Peterborough, Ontario. They had been fighting over mandates in their community, long before the

Convoy, and the entire municipal government attacked them, constantly. They lost everything, except their dignity. To me, they are a model of what it means to be a good citizen and to do what is necessary to protect your community. Even if it is the government you have to fight against.

The press conference ended, and I was demoralized and exhausted. Most of the people I had been working with, had either left or were in police custody. Keith and Eva were still in the city, but they were planning their exit from Ottawa as well.

The press conference and the phone call to the OPP that morning had no impact on police at that point. Anyone found inside the "red zone" was either ticketed or harassed by police. It was like watching hyenas attack their prey. They didn't move concrete barriers and they certainly didn't give anyone fuel.

Many of the Truckers chose to stay. Most left. Those who had their trucks impounded, paid thousands of dollars in fees and for damages to their trucks. The police routinely smashed truck windows and left the engines to run dry of fuel. It was a vindictive thing to do because many of the Truckers intentionally left their doors open to avoid this from happening. As the trucks sat in the impound lots, the insides filled with snow and water. It was vandalism that cost protesters thousands of dollars.

Many truck drivers were beaten when they surrendered to the police. An Eastern European Trucker named Csaba Vizi, who grew up in a communist country, was charged by the police and seen on video being badly beaten after he surrendered.

What I found most heartbreaking about that day was that

ordinary Canadians who digest mainstream media, didn't care that Canadians were being beaten and arrested for protesting. They didn't care about our Veterans. They only took interest when 280 of us had our bank accounts frozen. When these ordinary Canadians realized they could get their accounts frozen for wrong-think, only then did they care. Before that, they couldn't even be bothered to ask the simple question, "Why are people really protesting in Ottawa?"

But, as Decks told a lot of the Convoy that day, "The Government isn't going to kill you. You might get arrested and have a few broken bones, but it will show the world what Trudeau is really like and how far he's willing to go. Short-term pain for long-term gain."

He was right. Trudeau had shown the world just how far he was willing to go to destroy this country.

Chapter 18

Warrant Officer James Topp and Canada Marches

I first met Corporal James Topp in 1996 when I arrived in Meaford, Ontario, to start the Assault Pioneer Course. This was only the second time this training had been offered to reserve soldiers. During this course, we learned basic combat engineer skills, but as infantry soldiers. This was one of the best courses I'd ever done in the military. I had been interested in joining the regular army as an officer when I graduated from Construction Engineering Technology at Niagara College, for me, this course was a perfect chance to see if I was making a good decision about the engineers.

The majority of the sixteen candidates were reservists, except for James Topp and Jeff Donaldson. Both of them were regular force infantry soldiers from the Royal Canadian Regiment in Petawawa. James was also part of the Parachute Company and wore a maroon beret.

When you are a young reservist and you have to interact with the regular army guys, it can be a little intimidating. But, if you work hard, you can find someone willing to mentor you into becoming a better soldier – most times, but not always. There is friction between regular and reserve forces.

For some reason on that course, Jeff, James, and I stuck together and worked really well alongside each other. It's safe to say, the three of us were the biggest soldiers on that course, so we probably took on 50% of the work. As I spent more time with James, he shared some of his experiences of the year he spent in the former Bosnia Herzegovina in 1992 and '93.

James was there during the Medak Pocket when Canadian soldiers were sent into this area of Croatia to implement a ceasefire between the Croatians and Serbians fighting there. I remember him telling me that the first three months of this tour were boring. The following six months were absolutely terrifying and the last three months went back to being boring again. By this time in 1996, he had been affected by his experiences in that civil war, and it was having an impact on his personal life and to some extent his career. For a short time after that tour, he left the army, but within a year he re-enlisted.

Throughout the rest of his career, he did three more operational deployments and was on deployment during the 9/11 terrorist attacks. Following that deployment, he did two combat tours as a sniper in Afghanistan in a reconnaissance platoon, and another as the platoon Warrant Officer. In total, he has spent over two and a half years of his life on operational tours and in wartime.

When the Assault Pioneer course was complete, and to no one's surprise, James was the top candidate. I have always suspected that James has a photographic memory or very close to it. We would have tests almost daily on that course and it drove me crazy that he would spend about twenty minutes laying on his cot reading his notes and then declare it was time to go into town. The rest of us, me included, needed a lot more time to study. James also has an outstanding sense of humor, and he can make you laugh just with his facial expressions.

It would be some time before I would see James again, but we ran into each other occasionally when we were both posted to the Canadian Forces Base Petawawa in Ontario.

The year before the pandemic struck, James was still in the Regular Army but honorably retired while simultaneously part of a reserve unit in Chilliwack, BC. He took on a full-time position working for the RCMP as a Range Warden where he was looking after the shooting ranges for them. But because of the COVID-19 mandates that were imposed on federal employees, it meant he would be required to take the experimental COVID-19 injection or be simultaneously fired from the Canadian Army Reserves as well as his full-time civilian job with the RCMP. James chose his health and the constitutional rights he defended for twenty-seven years, over being violated by the Government.

As a result, he was put on unpaid leave by the RCMP and was given an ultimatum by the army to get injected or get out. Its interesting to me that in my twenty-five years of being a soldier, no one ever accused the Canadian Military of being loyal to its members!

On February 20th, 2022, after the second day of attacks by the police in Ottawa, James decided he would no longer sit idly by, doing nothing, while this country was being torn apart by the governments at every level.

While in uniform, he did a video explaining that he was about to walk across Canada as a form of protest regarding COVID-19 mandates. He started at the Terry Fox statue in Vancouver, with the intended goal to reach the Tomb of the Unknown Soldier in Ottawa. The trip would see him march, with a rucksack on his back, 4297 km/2670 mi, in 131 days. He was quickly joined by another reservist named Cristian George. This would be the beginning of "Canada Marches".

Not long after returning home from the Convoy, I saw the video James did, but I didn't recognize him until I heard him speak. Some of the other veterans I knew from the Convoy discussed what James was taking on and we agreed to help him in any way we could. By this time, Veterans for Freedom (V4F), had already been created and there was a strong appetite to support James.

As time when on, many of the veterans who attended the Convoy, found a way to get involved with Canada Marches. In many cases, they would physically show up to help on different legs of the journey. James and Cristian had acquired an RV with a trailer on the back. They used it as a mobile supply vehicle and HQ, but not for sleeping. Instead, they would stay in people's homes, businesses, and various community centers.

I finally got a chance to speak with James one night, to get a better idea of what he was doing and what he needed. However, right around that time, I decided to run as a candidate with the Ontario Party, in the upcoming Ontario Provincial election for Member of Provincial Parliament. That meant my time to help James would be very limited, but that was when V4F members stepped in and really made a difference.

Their goal was to help James find accommodations along the way, as well as to raise money for food and fuel. V4F had member veterans in the West and James was a long way away from reaching Ontario. The relationship between Canada Marches and V4F would only get stronger when James arrived in Ontario, as the bulk of our members were here, and Ottawa was the final destination on the journey.

In his travels, James had some great successes but also some incredibly disappointing obstacles to overcome. One of the things he was working on, through a courageous Member of the Federal Parliament, Dean Allison, was getting a meeting with Federal MPs. Dean and his staff worked hard on this. He was a Conservative MP near my home riding of Niagara West. I liked Dean because he had the guts to step up and do the right thing. It was Dean who arranged the meeting with James which was open to any member of Parliament who was interested in hearing what James had to say and who wanted to get involved.

I was campaigning until June 2nd, 2022, so my involvement was reduced to a weekly call with James just to stay in the loop. V4F had grown and was fully immersed in Canada Marches with some of our members joining James and Cristian for the entire Ontario leg of the journey.

The Ontario election was June 2nd and the only thing to mention is that I lost. Two days later, I was with the entire team of Canada Marches in Mattawa, Ontario. James kept an agonizing pace and was marching approximately 40 km/25 mi per day. I arrived late morning and decided to follow along until the day's marching was done. He had so many supporters come out, but traffic control was difficult, so safety for those wanting to meet him became an issue for the team. It amazed me that people would stop James in the middle of the road to take selfies with him and hand him money, but the excitement to meet him was overwhelming for many.

James had a real dilemma now and he needed to make a tough decision. The House of Commons was about to go on their summer recess, so the Members of Parliament would not be in Ottawa when he was due to arrive on June 30th. They were scheduled to leave almost two weeks before that. Dean Allison was helping to arrange a meeting with the MPs, but James wouldn't be there in time. He had developed a few courses of action to deal with this. The first one, which I hated the most, was for me to go in his place and have the meetings. I felt that I didn't deserve to take his spot but since he asked me, I would not refuse if that was his decision. I owed it to him to do the job. The other option, which he ultimately chose, was for him to halt the march and drive to Ottawa for two days of meetings and then return to where he left off and end the journey in Ottawa on the 30th. He requested that I join him in the meeting, as well as a very outspoken researcher, Paul Alexander who has a PhD in Evidence-Based Medicine.

On the 18th of June, Warrant Officer James Topp had succeeded where no one had in the previous two years of Covid-19 insanity. He got a meeting with the Government, or so we thought. It turns out that only some Conservative Members were available to attend. Not a single member of the Liberal Party or the other federal political parties attended. Not one.

On the morning of June 18th, Paul, James, and I met to discuss the plan. While we were preparing, I encouraged James to share with the MPs, his experiences in the former Yugoslavia and Medak Pocket and the comparisons he was seeing while walking across Canada, talking to Canadians. At the time he felt reluctant to mention it, as he wanted to stay on topic, but I thought it was important that he related what he saw in the early days of that civil war, to what Canadians were feeling now.

The intention was to conduct two sessions of the meeting and present a plan that James had come up with, to the members. What surprised me was how few MPs showed up. They were in the middle of a party leadership race so I knew some of them would be playing politics with James and others wouldn't. Of the leadership candidates, Dr. Leslyn Lewis was the only one to attend.

I was particularly frustrated by the inability of these people to pay attention to what James was saying. I looked around the room and more than half of them were on their smartphones and not paying any attention. As the moderator for this meeting, I asked if anyone would like to step out and tend to their phones because it didn't feel as though we had everyone's attention. Many of them came in and out of the room and then would have conversations with the person beside them. It was frustrating and embarrassing.

I should have known better, but my biggest frustration in the first meeting was that many of the MPs waited in line to meet James, take a selfie, and then immediately leave before the meeting began. For the second meeting, I didn't allow photos until the end of the meeting.

It was obvious that most of them couldn't care less about the reason for the meeting. It frustrated me because there was this attitude that James was fortunate to have met them. From my perspective, they should have been tripping over themselves to meet James, a man who had literally risked his life, on five operational tours for Canada. I've never been a fan of the phrase, "Thank you for your service," because, at times like this meeting, it's apparent it has become completely cliché. People love to give great speeches during Remembrance Day but when they have an opportunity to meet a real Combat Veteran, it's an entirely different interaction.

However, there were a few very sincere MPs. Bob Zimmer stood out as the most genuine of them all. MP Jeremy Patzer made a statement that we had allies within the Conservative Party, and I took his comments to be truthful and felt like a few of them really understood.

The one person who was glaringly absent, was the interim leader of the Conservative Party, Candice Bergen. To me, she had been walking a very fine line since taking over as leader during the Convoy, as she had taken a photo op with some Truckers and the next day, in the House of Commons, gave a speech telling us to go home for the sake of the economy. On one hand, she was supporting us, calling us patriotic, and on the other, she was telling us to leave. I recognized she was in a tough spot, but people prefer leaders with courage and conviction, not flip-flopping leaders who pander. I was frustrated because I couldn't help admiring how articulate she was, but I couldn't tell what side she was really on.

During our meeting, it was difficult to keep my cool at times. Between the MPs on their smartphones and the overall childish behavior of not all, but many in the group, I realized we were wasting our time. I felt like we had to say something to convey the seriousness of what James was hearing from Canadians, so I handed James a note suggesting again, that he talk about his time in Croatia. He really didn't want to do it, but I strongly encouraged him – and it was a mistake the media would make us pay for.

Reluctantly, James recounted an observation he made while in the Medak Pocket. As they went into this little village and saw the buildings full of bullet holes, he looked into the window of a home. Sitting on the table, was a full, uneaten meal. James observed that the people there were caught completely off guard and had no idea they were about to be attacked in their village, during dinner. He assumed it must have happened so fast that they abandoned their homes and ran for the adjacent hills to escape the attack. The point James was trying to convey to these MPs, was that the temperament here was getting very close to what he had experienced in that civil war, and he didn't want to see Canada do the same.

At the end of the afternoon, with the second meeting over, the mainstream media decided to surround us as we were walking to the door. We told them to wait to ask questions until we had our cameras set up to protect ourselves from their typical story manipulations. Surprisingly they waited, but it didn't make a difference. Their questions were very well structured to make us look as bad as possible. You could see they had a real sense of agitation about them, and they seemed like they were given instructions from their superiors, to discredit us.

William Diaz-Berthiaume, a young reporter from Rebel News, seemed to be the only person who stuck to asking factual questions that were absent of a malicious agenda.

What was frustrating to me was that they only asked James one question, before it became clear I was the one they were targeting. They kept asking me leading questions to frame a narrative that I was trying to incite civil war. The error I made was getting engrossed in trying to answer the actual question and losing sight of the bigger picture they were trying to frame.

Thankfully, James saw what they were trying to do and shut the interview down. I was extremely appreciative that he did, but

I realize because I failed to see the bigger agenda, my actions had unintentionally assisted the legacy media in successfully creating a negative story about why we were there to meet with the members of parliament.

Of course, the media was incredibly disrespectful to both the members of parliament who agreed to attend the meetings, as well as the purpose we were all there for. It was just as much of a media smear campaign against the members of Conservative Parliament, as it was for me and by extension James, because of what we were trying to do.

After we met with the Federal Conservatives, James went back to where he had paused his walk. He completed the journey and triumphantly marched into the city of Ottawa with a few minor incidents on June 30th, 2022.

There were a few thousand people who joined him on his final 22 km/13.5 mi leg into the city. Veterans For Freedom provided traffic safety and acted as security, because there was a group of dubious counter-protesters who had announced on social media, that they planned to disrupt Canada Marches, on the last day. Just to highlight a terrible example of the divide between Canadians, this group of counter-protesters claimed to be military veterans!

James's speech, at the National War Memorial, was absolutely incredible. There is a section of his speech that really stuck with me.

"Seeing something that is wrong, speaking up, and doing

something about it.

I displayed a little bit of courage; it wasn't something I was born with. I learned it from them, the Snr NCOs and Officers I worked with. I learned it from the Police officers. I wasn't born courageous, I learned it from you!

We have freedom here in this country, but it's slowly being siphoned away – but we're going to do something about it, like we have since January.

So Canada... where do we go from here?

Many have lost hope, feel lost, and are justifiably angry. However, many more have taken this pain and instead risen up to birth a movement, built on the sacred values of freedom, unity, and sovereignty.

Discern, assemble, organize, and plan – but do all these peacefully and with the knowledge that you are standing up for the Truth. Standing up for our COUNTRY, which was built brick by brick by people who honored freedom and stood for democracy, and allowed any to speak, even when they disagreed with them.

It's not easy to be brave... but it is always worth it. Face your demons and overcome your fears."

The next day, Canada Day, I was asked to give a speech in front of Parliament Hill. I spent all day writing the speech and preparing for what I wanted to say, with the help of my good friend James Poloso, who was producing the docuseries on the Convoy called 'Trucking for Freedom'.

As I arrived at the location to give my speech, there was a negative vibe in the air, and I felt very uneasy about my surroundings. There was security at the two entrances to the main grounds on Parliament Hill, and someone saw me get in line to be searched. She approached me and said she knew who I was, and that she was really disappointed in me for getting in that search line. I have to say, her attitude and demeanor were pretty insulting, and I had no concerns about living with her disappointment.

After a lot of very unnecessary drama, I was really frustrated with a portion of the crowd, and also the by-law enforcement people. Both groups were seeming to do everything they could to antagonize each other and at one point, By-Law Officers had gone from threatening to confiscate the audio equipment and charge me to handing me the microphone to get the crowd to calm down and move back a bit, which I did.

When it was my turn to speak, I just couldn’t deliver the speech I’d written. Instead, I told the crowd they were never going to get what they wanted from the police if they kept antagonizing them. To be fair, many police in this country deserve the disrespect and distrust of the public for what they did to us during Covid. But not all of them do.

There were thousands of police advocating in one way or another for us and in many cases at great personal cost. But a section of this crowd didn’t want to hear it and the more I spoke, the more they shouted over me.

It's not a day I’m proud of, for my own choice of words, but I stand by my sentiment. Out of frustration, I finally relented and stopped talking.

As a side note, the difficulty of putting yourself out there is that you are always susceptible to attacks, even from your own team. For example, this day would later come back to bite me in the form of a personal attack from the leader of the New Blue political party in Ontario, at the POEC. The New Blue supposedly supported the Convoy mission of ending all mandates, but apparently, they weren't fans of Tom Marazzo.

A video excerpt from my speech, which was taken out of context, was shown during a Convoy participant's testimony. No one understood what the relevance of my speech on Canada Day had to the POEC, as the POEC was meant to examine the actions of the federal cabinet.

These attacks from supporters of that party were common and started almost immediately after the Freedom Convoy ended. One of their candidates even tweeted there were rumors of false leaders in the Convoy, and that I was a fake. Why? To me, they simply took yet another opportunity to come after me, five months later. All because I had endorsed the Ontario Party, not the New Blue.

After my Canada Day speech, I did receive some supportive messages from people who understood what I was trying to say. But overall, it was a disaster and I regret accepting the invitation to speak. Since that day, I have never participated in any outdoor live events and have no desire to do so ever again. I have no interest in engaging with intoxicated people walking around draped in "Fuck Trudeau" flags, screaming "Freedom", while expecting to be taken seriously by anyone. If we want to be heard, we need to be better and not act like the fringe that the PM and media accuse us of being.

After what happened with the media on June 18th and then my Canada Day speech, it started to feel like everything I was doing was more harmful than helpful. Good people were doing their best and somehow, I was making it harder for them. I decided the best thing to do was to take a break and spend some time alone on my land.

Other than an amazing trip to Alberta, I lived alone on my land for most of July, August, and September. I knew I would be returning to Ottawa for the POEC, but it had been delayed until October.

On Monday the 10th of October, Keith Wilson texted me and asked me how soon I could get to Ottawa. I was there the next morning!

Chapter 19

Public Order Emergency Commission

What's important to understand about the Public Order Emergency Commission (POEC), is the fact that when the Government of Canada invokes The Emergencies Act, by law under Section 63 of The Emergencies Act itself, the government has 360 days from the date of revocation of the Act, to submit a report to the government as to the reasons they invoked it. So, once it was invoked, Keith Wilson and Eva Chipiuk both reviewed The Emergencies Act and knew that in the future we would all be going back to Ottawa, but we didn't know in what capacity.

As part of the process set out by the government in the terms of reference, interested parties had the opportunity to apply to the Commission for standing, in order to testify or participate. In my case it was fairly obvious I would be selected, as well as other more notable participants of the Convoy, along with some less notable individuals. As expected, I was subpoenaed to testify. Keith Wilson was as well, and this created a difficult situation for all of us.

The reason Keith was subpoenaed by the Commission counsel, is because he was the head lawyer advising us during the Convoy. He had the key evidence about the deal with the city and how the police and federal government blocked that deal from going through. This was very important to be explained at the Inquiry because it showed The Emergencies Act was not needed: the borders were open and there was a deal that was working in Ottawa. Unfortunately, being subpoenaed meant he was a witness, so he was excluded from being our legal counsel at the Inquiry.

Under section 62 of The Emergencies Act, there is an opportunity for a judicial review - a process by which courts make sure the decisions of administrative bodies are fair, reasonable, and lawful. It is similar to proceedings in a lawsuit. In this case, a plaintiff files a judicial review against a government and there's only a short window of opportunity to file it.

A judicial review was filed by both Eddie Cornell and Vince

Gircys and they retained the services of lawyers Brendan Miller and Bath-Shéba Vandenberg. What's interesting about this is both Section 62 and 63 were happening simultaneously and neither group of lawyers were working together on those specific legal proceedings. Keith called me early in the summer of 2022 and explained his situation. He recommended we bring in additional lawyers to help with the Inquiry. He spoke to me and had several phone calls with the members of the Freedom Corp. Board and Danny Bulford, with the same recommendation for all of us. He called because he was thoroughly impressed with Brendon Miller and the things that he had already discovered while preparing for Section 62. Although Keith has many more years of experience than Brendon, he was thoroughly impressed with Brendan's ability to dissect everything that went on in Ottawa with the Convoy, in such a short amount of time.

While we were at the POEC, Brendan apologized to us because it turns out that in the beginning, he wasn't a supporter of the Convoy and thought we were all exactly what the media had said we were. His involvement in the POEC completely changed his opinion about us and the federal government. I consider Brendan a lifelong friend.

Keith's recommendation, if we agreed, was to ask the JCCF if they would hire Brendon and Bath-Shéba to join the legal team representing Freedom Corp. at the POEC. With funding, they were hired. Additionally, because we needed Keith to tell the Inquiry the details of what happened, we decided to waive attorney-client privilege so he could provide unguarded testimony.

I spent much of that summer living off-grid on my land, but in July, Keith asked me if I would be willing to come to Alberta for a couple of days to prepare for the POEC, which was supposed to start in September. So, I made the long, two-and-a-half day drive to Keith's. I put the seats down in the back of my Honda and slept each night on a foldable six-inch thick mattress. Some people reading this might consider that a little bit rough, but from my perspective, if this had been a military trip it would have been the lap of luxury, so I didn't mind it one bit. Overall, I have to say I thoroughly enjoyed the trip, because I got to see so much of Canada that I had never experienced before. The thought of the Convoy driving from out West, all the way to Ottawa, was constantly on my mind.

Being at Keith's for the Inquiry preparation meetings was the first time many of us had seen each other since February. It was like a family reunion. During this prep time, I was introduced to the abbreviation, "IMVE", which is Ideologically Motivated Violent Extremism". From my perspective, this described the Liberal Party of Canada perfectly, but then I realized that is what they were going to call us!

The sticky part of being at Keith's for all of us was having any form of contact with Tamara because she had already needlessly been arrested and spent twenty-five days in jail for appearing in a photograph with me. The entire re-arrest of Tamara, on a Canada-wide warrant, for breach of a bail condition was one of the most shameful things I've ever seen the so-called justice system do to one of its citizens.

Because of what had already happened to Tamara, we made

alternative arrangements for her participation in the POEC prep meetings with the lawyers, so she wouldn't be targeted again.

Every year the JCCF gives out an award called the George Jonas Freedom Award and the recipient, for 2022, was Tamara. Her bail conditions state that she is to have no contact with me and several other people, many of them she doesn't even know. The caveat is that we can be together only if we are in the presence of our lawyers. Well, the very law firm that represents both of us, the JCCF, is the one who sponsored the dinner and the award.

The head of the JCCF, John Carpay, sat at a table with us and many of the staff lawyers we interacted with were there too. Seated directly behind Tamara was her criminal lawyer, Diane Magas. To say that she was not in the presence of her lawyers and that she deserved to be arrested on a Canada-wide warrant, at her home in Alberta, is absolutely grotesque and it demonstrates how far our government is willing to go to silence people that oppose their dictates. Canada-wide warrants are only issued for dangerous criminals, not the perception of a bail breach.

Regardless of the absurdity, Tamara is the vulnerable one, so we always took extra precautions. I have never been alone with Tamara and have always been in the presence of our lawyers when with her, especially, during the POEC.

One of Tamara's additional bail conditions was that she was prevented from being in the downtown area of the city of Ottawa. However, this put her in direct violation of the subpoena she was given, to appear at the POEC, because it was being held in the very area that she was prevented from being in. Potentially she could have been arrested had she abided by the subpoena. Conversely, had she not abided by the subpoena, she could also have been arrested.

You would think the Ottawa crown attorney who was targeting Tamara would understand this simple dilemma. Instead, he chose to threaten Tamara with re-arrest if she attended the POEC. The situation became so ridiculous that Brendan Miller spoke to the Commission counsel and informed them, that the Ottawa City crown attorney was threatening to arrest Tamara in Ottawa, right inside the building where the POEC was being held. Thankfully, Commission counsel notified the crown attorney that if any police officer attempted to apprehend Tamara at the POEC, that police officer would be arrested for contempt of court and interfering in a judicial proceeding.

At one point, Tamara was out in front of the building where we were housed during the Commission, for a cigarette break, when three Ottawa police officers approached her and warned her that had she stepped beyond the property line of the building they were there to arrest her. This was beyond ridiculous when you consider she had to travel from the place we were staying, to the building where the POEC was being held. It turns out that a busybody in our building, recognized Tamara and called the police. They were more than happy to harass her at any opportunity, so three police officers, all of the rank of Sergeant, sat out front of our building in three different police SUVs.

Finally, Brendan was able to discuss the situation with Tamara's criminal lawyer, Lawrence Greenspon, who got Tamara's bail conditions amended to stop the threats and the harassment. But again, Tamara and I were never left alone together, because we knew they were potentially watching her every move. With all the mainstream media around, there was no way any of us were going to take a chance with Tamara's freedom. Even during the daily testimony of the POEC, we were never alone in each other's company. The joke became that the lawyers were the most expensive babysitters and photobombers known to mankind.

In September we found out the Commission was going to be delayed one full month, because of a health-related issue of Commissioner Rouleau. The POEC began on the 13th of October and ran until the 25th of November 2022. On the Monday before the POEC started, Keith called me and asked me how soon I could be in Ottawa. Given that I haven't been employed since getting fired from my teaching job, I told him I could be there whenever he needed me. He said,"Good, I'll see you here in Ottawa tomorrow!"

I spent the rest of the day packing and preparing for an unspecified period in Ottawa, for the second time in the same year. It was an unusual request, but Keith asked if I could bring a coffee maker and a whiteboard. What's funny was that I still had one of the whiteboards and one of the coffee makers, that we used at the Arc Hotel during the Convoy! Yes, bizarrely nostalgic, but it felt good bringing those items back to Ottawa. The plan was for me to stay in one of the bedrooms of the apartment Keith was in, and Tamara stayed with Eva in her apartment in the same building, so we had to be extremely diligent to never be left alone with each other.

All the other lawyers had accommodations in that same building, and they typically used Keith's apartment as the main workplace after hours. The reason Keith wanted me to stay there for the duration of the POEC, was to help him with interviews and social media content because other people had bail conditions and they were prevented from speaking to the media about any Convoy-related issues. Keith was concerned that if he and Eva were the only ones doing interviews, they would oversaturate the media and people would stop paying attention to what was going on.

As a rule, Brendan and Bath-Shéba did not do any type of media during the POEC, because Keith didn't want any accidental missteps that would have to be dealt with during the proceedings. Since I didn't have any bail conditions or a gag order, I did much of the media and I was also invited by Rebel News to provide daily commentary on what transpired at the POEC each day.

I have to say it was incredibly difficult to sit there in the audience, day after day, listening to politicians, other government officials, and police constantly using very defamatory vocabulary to describe what happened during the Convoy. For example, the number of times it was called an "illegal occupation", or we were referred to as "occupiers", was incredibly difficult to sit through. It was like being a fly on the wall when people are talking about you behind your back. But, then again, we knew we would get our chance to testify and tell our perspective of the experience.

During the first three and a half weeks or so, we were satisfied with the way the Commission was going. We were definitely trying to manage our expectations, but we were somewhat surprised, almost to the point of confusion, that the Commission Counsel and Commissioner Rouleau appeared to be doing an impartial job and were focusing on facts. But all that changed about the 5th week, unfortunately right after I had given some public statements saying that the Commission was doing a good job.

As we got closer and closer to the final week, our team of lawyers were struggling with the amount of information the Justice Department, or as I like to refer to them as, the Justin Department, was dumping on the Commission.

The way the proceedings were laid out was, if you knew you were going to cross-examine somebody on a Thursday, you had to have all the documentation you were going to question the witness on, submitted to the Commission's database three days prior to cross-examining your witness. For example, when it was my turn to be cross-examined on November 2nd, all of the evidence that any of the legal teams wanted to question me on, had to be submitted to the database three days prior, so that I and our lawyers could go through the material.

But what was very difficult for our team, was that the lawyers for the federal government, started routinely dumping thousands and thousands of documents into the database. Nobody could possibly go through all of them, and often they didn't meet the three days prior deadline, making it even more difficult to get through the material. It wouldn't surprise me if Justin Trudeau's tax returns since 1986, or the Trudeau family turkey recipe, or something equally ridiculous were in that pile of evidence.

However, what became very suspect to Brendon, and the lawyers, was all of the redacted information from the government. Trudeau publicly stated this would be an open and transparent Commission, yet his lawyers were submitting heavily redacted documents. At one point the Minister of Justice, David Lametti, also refused to waive attorney-client privilege and at some point, there was also cabinet confidence being cited. The closer we got to the Prime Minister's testimony, scheduled for the final day of the POEC, the more the stonewalling increased.

When Marco Mendicino testified and it was our turn to ask questions, Brendan Miller had been removed from the proceedings earlier in the day by Justice Rouleau, so Keith delicately stepped in, because he was a witness and not counsel at the POEC. Keith explained to the Commission that we were not prepared to cross-examine the witness.

"Sir, we're not in a position to proceed with cross at this time. There are two reasons. One is the federal government has disclosed over a week ago an extension volume of documents that are highly redacted. It is obvious from the face of the documents that they don't meet the criteria for lawful redactions. A motion was made last week for those redactions to be lifted. The submissions closed on Thursday evening. We still have no ruling; a number of days have passed. For the cross-examination and the discovery of truth process to be valid and effective, the parties require access to the documents; we don't have that. So we would appreciate some indication as to when the Commission is actually going to rule on that and hopefully compel the proper disclosure of the record so that cross-examinations can be effective. I emphasize that these documents are not related to

future witnesses, but present witnesses, so we're making the process inefficient, with all due respect, by not allowing the parties to have access to unredacted documents. The second reason we're not in a position to proceed with our cross-examination at this time with this witness is our lead counsel, Mr. Brendan Miller, who had prepared for the cross, as you know, sir, has been removed by the room by you when he was raising a motion to find a way around the absence of a ruling on the redaction. So, we're just not in a position to proceed on cross, sir."

The reason Brendan had been removed from the POEC that day, was because he had filed two separate motions asking for evidence to be unredacted. Eight days had passed, and Rouleau still had not made a ruling on the motions, which was well outside the time Brendan needed to act on the evidence he wanted to see, to cross-examine relevant witnesses.

Before the first morning break, Brendan asked for the Commissioner to make an oral ruling on his new motion to allow a new witness, who happened to be sitting in the room at that moment, to testify. Rouleau asked Brendan if he had submitted this new motion in writing, but Brendan replied, "I didn't expect that we would have the opportunity" because we just learned about this witness. Of course, Rouleau refused to allow it and Brendan responded with, "We're given fifteen minutes to cross-examine, elicit relevant material evidence, and we have relevant and material witnesses here. The Government of Canada has redacted without lawful authority all of these statements from these staffers and have suppressed records."

To everyone's frustration, Rouleau was more concerned about the process, which he wasn't following properly, and the schedule than he was about his mandate of getting to the truth.

After a fifteen minute break, Brendan didn't want to let it go so he was standing at the podium, waiting for the Commission to resume. Brendan immediately started, and this time it was more heated, with the two of them talking over each other. Brendan started with, "Your counsel has advised you that, I know you've directed you wanted the application" and Rouleau cuts him off, "I'm sorry, I'm speaking. The application, if you want to do it, you've been advised it's to be done in writing, not in the middle of the presentation." Brendan was not going to give up, made a calculated move, and threw an elbow. "Sir, we've filed two motions in writing at your direction that you've refused to rule on, with respect to the redaction of documents from the Government of Canada that has not been ruled on, has been filed for days."

Fortunately, or unfortunately, depending on how you look at it, Rouleau decided to have Brendan removed and said, "I will take a break while you're asked to leave. I will return in five minutes. If security could deal with counsel." As politely as they could, the security team escorted Brendan outside.

Luckily, Brendan was allowed back inside the POEC that same afternoon. And the impact was that Brendan never had any more issues getting his motions heard or ruled on. The one thing I can tell you about Brendan Miller is that he will fight to the death for what he believes is right. In this case, he had to go up against a judge while being live-streamed on the internet with full MSM coverage.

I saw firsthand how extremely exhausting it is for lawyers to do cross-examinations back-to-back, day-after-day because of the intense number of hours it takes to prepare for every person they examine. While Brendan was getting a lot of help, he was the one person doing most of the cross-examining for our team. Because of this, he was getting badly burnt out. Not only that, the rest of the team was burning out too, but they didn't have to do the cross-examinations, which was a huge layer of additional stress.

Because Brendan had already been removed once in his effort to uncover the truth, his stress level more than doubled. There were many nights he would be up extremely late or into the early morning and some nights he didn't sleep at all. Those long days and even longer nights were exhausting for him, but Brendan was always on his game and brought it every single day without fail!

When it was Brendan's turn to go up to the podium to do his cross-examination, we came to refer to it as, "Miller Time." Somebody in one of the chat groups made a hilarious meme, with the Miller Beer logo imposed on the big computer screen at the front of the POEC room.

I think one of the best cross-examinations of all, was when Brendan cross-examined Chrystia Freeland. The irony was that he was at his most exhausted point but pulled off the most brilliant cross-examination I witnessed to date.

The final person to be cross-examined was Justin Trudeau, the

Prime Minister of Canada. For him, the team came up with a drastically different strategy. The night before that cross examination, it was safe to say that Brendan Miller was exhausted beyond recovery. What he pulled off in all those weeks was incredible. I believe he could have continued because he's a true legal warrior, but Brendan had taken his line of arguments as far as he possibly could. We would need a new tactic for the next day's witness and that was when we decided to have somebody else cross-examine the Prime Minister.

Unfortunately, Keith was prevented from cross-examining Trudeau because he was a witness. That left Bath-Shéba or Eva. It was late, around 9:30 or 10 p.m. and the collective decision was to put Eva in, to do the cross-examination. The goal was not to get him to make any admission about why he invoked The Emergencies Act. Instead, we intended to expose the hypocrisies and to have the entire freedom movement see him face the consequences of his actions.

While the rest of the team worked to come up with a list of questions they wanted to ask Trudeau, I stayed away from Keith's apartment, with Brendan. It's safe to say it was a very late night for everybody. But that late night definitely paid off.

When we arrived at the POEC the next morning, I can only imagine how Eva's stomach was feeling, but she is an exceptional lawyer and great under pressure, but cross-examining the Prime Minister of Canada is a unique situation, especially under the circumstances!

We had a list of the other legal teams who would be cross-examining Justin Trudeau and approximately how much time they would each be given. As I was sitting there, I did a quick calculation and realized that Eva would not be crossing him until after lunch. I thought this was very good because it gave us more prep time and to get a feel for what the rest of the room was like. We could also gauge the mood of Rouleau in terms of how far he'd let Eva push Trudeau.

During the lunch break, I sat with Eva and Bath-Shéba, and we rehearsed. I drew the short straw and had to pretend I was Justin Trudeau. The role was easy for me because I didn't have to answer any questions, and I hummed and hawed quite a bit, and I had to try to stall for time, which is what we expected he would do. The important part of that was to estimate how long it would take Eva to get through all of her questions. As it turned out, we had too many questions, so Eva had to prioritize a little more because she truly needed to get to the final question. It was like a comedian leading the audience through a story to develop the punchline, and this is exactly what Eva needed to do.

There was an occasion during Eva's cross-examination where the live audience members became vocally upset with Trudeau's answers. She asked him, "A number of people have testified in this Inquiry referencing your widely published comments and calling the unvaccinated racists and misogynists. And we have heard testimony in this Inquiry about how some of your officials wanted to label protesters as terrorists. Would you agree with me that one of the most important roles of a Prime Minister is to unite Canadians and not divide them by engaging in name-calling?"

He literally said, on the witness stand, "I did not call people who were unvaccinated names," at which point, Rouleau had to regain order in the room.

Afterward, many people wondered why Trudeau wasn't charged with perjury for lying under oath, but somebody much smarter than me, could probably write an entire book about the lying that politicians in the government get away with.

For Eva's final question, she asked Justin Trudeau, "My last question, Mr. Prime Minister. When did you and your government start to become so afraid of your own citizens?" And once again, Rouleau had to regain control of the room.

In the early days of the Commission, I was seeing a lot of comments on social media, with people constantly asking the same questions to me and the lawyers. They were very passionate about the types of questions they wanted answered. Even in my case, I kept trying to convince Keith and Brendan to ask the witnesses, "Why, or when, did they decide they would not speak to any of us during the Convoy? Why did they refuse to have any dialogue with us?"

Finally, Keith and Brendan sat me down in the apartment one night and told me that those questions were irrelevant because they don't get to the heart of the matter. On average, they only got about ten minutes to cross-examine each witness and they were not going to waste their time on questions that were not relevant to the proceedings. That was very frustrating for me because I wanted them to ask many of the witnesses my most important question, about them refusing to talk to the protesters.

Here's the issue, and I had been told this previously by Bath-Shéba, but given that I'm not a lawyer, it really didn't sink in. In order for the government to invoke The Emergencies Act, they have to see clear evidence of one of the four conditions of Section 2 of the CSIS Act. If anyone of those four conditions is met, the government can invoke The Emergencies Act. That's the true heart of the matter. Brendan, during his opening remarks on day one, stated clearly as he walked through each of the four conditions, that there would be no testimony spoken, that would justify the invocation of The Emergencies Act because invocation clearly did not meet any of the conditions of Section 2 of the CSIS Act.

Throughout the entire commission, Brendan focused on this fact with several very key witnesses, most notably Superintendent Pat Morris from the Ontario Provincial Police. Superintendent Morris confirmed that the conditions were not met, as did the head of CSIS David Vigneault. This was also confirmed by so many high-ranking government officials who testified, that when the lawyer for the JCCF, Hatim Kheir, was walking the head of CSIS through the four conditions, even the Commissioner, Justice Rouleau himself, said the following statement, "Yeah, although you could have skipped (a), (b), (c), (d). It's been testified to, many times that it wasn't met, but go ahead."

The Commissioner himself, on record, admitted that it was already established that the government did not meet any of the conditions under the CSIS Act, Section 2. I looked around the room in shock and thought that's it, it's game over, he just admitted it. I was looking for a reaction from everybody else in the room, and it was as if I was the only person who heard it. What's interesting to me, was that there was no reaction at all from anyone. That was the moment I thought there was a chance that Rouleau would produce a report that clearly stated the Government of Canada did not meet the very high threshold to invoke The Emergencies Act. However, my faith in these proceedings and Justice Rouleau was completely misplaced.

We later heard testimony from Jody Thomas, the National Security and Intelligence Adviser to the Federal Government, that they interpreted the Act very differently. To explain this absurdity, Keith Wilson likes to use the analogy, "Imagine you get pulled over by a police officer for speeding when the speed is clearly posted. The police officer informs you that you were pulled over for exceeding the posted limit which is against the law. But you turn to the police officer, and say yes officer, but that's not how I interpret the law in terms of speeding under the Highway Traffic Act." That’s exactly what Jody Thomas had done.

We waited almost until the last day before the deadline to hear the results of the final report from the POEC. I have a severe dislike of bullying and the concept of fairness is a righteous value I hold dearly. I know sometimes I am very naïve when it comes to my perception of how the world should be, versus our current reality. One thing I have come to believe over the last three years is that this country is either led through incompetence or corruption, and the results of the report were devastatingly disappointing, in terms of how corrupt this government actually is.

On the day the report was released, Justice Rouleau gave a public statement, "After careful reflection, I have concluded that the very high threshold required for the invocation of the Act, was met."

Chapter 20

Final Thoughts

I was the very last person to leave the Arc Hotel because I was there all day on February 20th. Everyone was gone and no one was allowed inside the "Red Zone" that had been set up by the police. I was sitting in the 2nd story window, of the Arc Hotel conference room when I saw Decks walking toward the Arc Hotel from the alley that connected to the Sheraton Hotel, one street north. As soon as he left the alley and headed onto Slater, he immediately turned east and saw a crowd of police harassing people, in front of the Arc Hotel. I thought for sure, the police were on their way into the hotel for whoever was left inside. Lucky for me, they never entered the hotel.

I cleaned out as much of the two conference rooms as I could fit into my SUV, and eventually met up with a group of people outside of the downtown core, where we stayed for the night.

I spent my final night in Ottawa, with Leanne Carter, Decks, Vickie, and Chantel. After the Convoy, very sadly for all of us, Chantel developed a brain tumor, and it took her life within weeks. It sent a wave of sorrow through those who worked with Chantel at the Convoy.

As I drove the two hours home, I was exhausted and numb. During the Convoy, my daughter and her mother were supposed to come to Ottawa in the middle of the second week, but because I was so sick, we decided to postpone a week and try again. I wanted them both to experience what it was truly like. Unfortunately, because Trudeau invoked the EA, we decided the situation was too unpredictable for my daughter. But it was an experience I wish she would have had.

My son, sixteen at the time, who doesn't live with me, didn't know I was at the Convoy. I found out afterward, that he didn't support it and we could never understand why, since he's not interested in the news or politics. His mother, who was a huge supporter of the Convoy, made me tell him I was there after I got home. He wasn't happy about it then, but we're good now!

Not long after the Convoy was over, someone said to me, "Why didn't you get those people out of there a week earlier? You knew they were going to get beaten. Everyone knew they were going to get beaten!" My response was one of surprise, to say the least, "You are grossly overestimating my influence with these people. They weren't going to leave just because Tom Marazzo said so."

At first, I just let the comment go but after about a month, that thought started to fester, and self-doubt started to creep deeply into my head. Depression, coupled with constant attacks from other Convoy participants, lasted mostly until the end of the POEC.

I will likely never stop thinking about what I could have done differently to avoid that treatment from happening. I often wonder what I missed that could have made a difference. Yes, there are many things I could and should have done differently.

The idea to consolidate as much as possible onto Wellington, that I put forward within hours of my first day in Ottawa, was very controversial. Many people, including the veterans, felt it weakened us tactically. It did and I knew it did, but I believed if we could have had everything on Trudeau's doorstep, it would have strengthened us strategically. I always believed the trade-off was worth it, especially since we were not there to engage in combat with anyone. Seeking a tactical advantage is something you would do if you had the intent of engaging in real combat. But we had no interest at all in such things, so tactics were not my concern. A solid strategy to get a dialogue going with the Liberals was where our focus always was.

It wasn't until we were halfway through the POEC that I finally realized, no matter what we would have done, Justin Trudeau wanted to have a violent crackdown on anyone who didn't agree with him. It didn't matter what we did, his Cabinet wanted their own "Tiananmen Square" moment, so they collectively tried to make us into their own "January 6th" from the USA the previous year.

The day after Justin Trudeau ended The Emergencies Act, he refocused his attention on the war between Russia and Ukraine. The vast majority of Canadians are supporters of the Ukrainian Government, although they are not part of NATO and are in fact, a former mortal enemy of the West from the Cold War era.

There were reports of the post-2014 Ukrainian government's problematic relations with extreme right-wing groups and neo-Nazi parties. In the context of the Russian invasion, this has become an incendiary element on both sides of the propaganda war, with Russia exaggerating it as a pretext for war and the West trying to sweep it under the carpet.

These same Canadians, who wanted to see me, and my unvaccinated children put into concentration camps, are now the morally virtuous saviors of democracy in Eastern Europe, while simultaneously not even able to find the country of Ukraine on a map! We are arming and funding the Ukrainians for one reason, and it's not for democracy. It is because our Deputy Prime Minister's family is Ukrainian. Her maternal grandparents immigrated to Alberta in 1939. Her mother returned to Ukraine as a Canadian-trained lawyer who founded the Ukrainian Legal Foundation, which helped the Ukrainian Independence movement. Halyna Chomiak Freeland helped draft the inaugural Ukrainian Constitution.

Ironically, I highlight this because our Deputy Prime

Minister's mother was a freedom fighter in Ukraine, like many of us here in Canada.

Under the current Liberal Government, or what I refer to as The Four Horsemen of the Liberal Apocalypse - Trudeau, Freeland, Mendocino, and Lametti, Canada has become an embarrassment internationally, because of their acts of tyranny. The same goes for Australia and New Zealand. For me, it raises the question, "What was truly going on all these years - before the Liberals finally showed us how corrupt our country is?"

Since the Convoy, things have not become much better but at least we're not still being forced to wear useless face masks in public. The Ontario Government has made it a crime to protest with a vehicle, near critical infrastructure. "Informed consent" is still being widely ignored by doctors. Those brave medical professionals who didn't take the injection and were fired, have not been hired back. Instead, our provincial government has hired foreign nurses to take their jobs.

The POEC cost taxpayers about $20 million and it was a whitewash as expected since the judge was a long-standing Liberal supporter.

A very courageous group of Canadians created something called the National Citizen's Inquiry. They funded the entire thing from donations and went across Canada to hear the real stories of what each level of Government has done to this country, due to Covid-19 actions. It is a Court of Public Opinion, and it matters!

Wokeism is a direct threat to the very fabric of what it means to be a family, and the public is again at odds with politicians over it.

The Canadian Armed Forces is at its lowest strength, probably since its post WWII drawdown. Morale is lower than it has ever been because of the illegal order issued by the Chief of Defense Staff to mandate Covid-19 experimental injections. As of the writing of this book, there is a Mass Tort filed with over 300 military members against the Government. The military is no longer combat-effective, and we are defenseless while our Prime Minister is trying to start a war with Russia. At least our military members are all "woke"!

The Convoy is long over, but I've had to rebuild my life almost every three months, and it's been very difficult each time.

I ran for provincial office with the Ontario Party, led by Derrek Sloan on June 2, 2022. I lost, and Ontario voters rewarded their domestic abuser, Doug Ford, with an even larger majority government than what he already had at the start of the pandemic.

I have been called a terrorist and an insurrectionist, as well as a hero, and a patriot. I am none of those things - but I am a father. That's the only title I am happy to be.

During the Convoy, I was slightly concerned about what my former colleagues in the military might think about me. I expected a lot of mixed reactions and calls for me to lose my pension, etc. But, all but one person ignored my existence. While I was at the Convoy, I was absolutely thrilled that one of my former commanding officers, LCol (Ret'd) Michael Southorn, emailed me with a letter of support. This was one of the biggest boosts for me during my time there. There were very few COs I respected in the military, and he was at the top of that list.

A few weeks before the POEC, Mike and I met, and he helped me process some of the mental issues I was having. One of them was trying to understand what "Tom Marazzo" had now become. Never in my life had I desired any form of notoriety, other than wanting to be known as a great software teacher. Yet here I was, making the news. I assumed that I had about a two-week shelf life and the attention would disappear. That's not exactly how it turned out. During my conversation with Mike, he said to me, "Don't be a Guru, just be an example of someone willing to stand up for what you believe." This simple, yet typical insight from Mike, was exactly what I needed to hear. This has been my mantra ever since the day of that conversation, and I only hope to inspire more people to set the same example and I'm using social media to do it.

I believe Western Civilization is in very deep trouble and quite possibly we're at the beginning of the end of life, as we know it. I don't mean that on an apocalyptic level, but on a spiritual and moral level. Too much has been exposed, in terms of government corruption and incompetence to ever go back to the lives we once had. We cannot un-ring the bell.

I'm relieved to say I can still go anywhere I want and have never been recognized unless it's at a freedom-related event. Most of the others can't say that, especially Chris Barber and Tamara Lich. I'm relieved because Canada has become so polarized that I'm terrified someone who hates me for participating in the Convoy will make their feelings known in front of my innocent children.

I wrote and distributed this message to all of the Convoy on the final day of February 19th and I'm putting it in this book because I believe much of it is still very relevant today, given the current state of Canada and the number of people I know who have chosen to leave.

"To all fellow Canadian Patriots in our FreedomConvoy2022.

We have not lost this Battle and the war is far from over.

As one of the volunteers helping every day to win this fight, I can assure you that we're winning. No matter how it looks, we never had the option to lose. Our children are counting on us.

We are not the government and will not tell you what to do or think.

The choice to stay or to leave is yours and yours alone.

If you leave, chin up, shoulders back, heads held high. You have done your part with distinction and honor.

If you choose to stay, I fear that you will not be in a position to fight another day if you lose everything.

This is one battle, in a sustained war. We need warriors for the next battle too.

I will not ask you to stay. I will not ask you to leave.

You make a decision that is right for you and your family.

You have, by now, been given alternate places to temporarily relocate, while we regroup and find a way forward.

I have been in discussions, through back channels to start discussions with the Government. I do not know if that will be successful, but I must try to advance our cause by all means available.

This is an individual and family decision.

God bless you all."

Unfortunately, the back-channeling I was trying to do was a complete dead end, if not a total waste of time. I still had to try.

I have often reflected on why I got that call on the morning of January 30th, 2022. I know smarter and more experienced retired officers, who may have done a much better job than me. But, for some reason, I'm the one who got the call and so be it.

I went because I felt a very profound sense of duty to fight for the future of my two children. That's the only reason I went.

It was, and still is, for them!

Donations and Well Wishes

My sincerest thanks to the financial donors listed, to the many who donated anonymously, as well as for the blessings, prayers, and well wishes I received daily on our funding campaign, via email and on social media. Your heart felt generosity has not only been monetary but spiritually uplifting as you've given me the gift of time, allowing me to fully devote myself to this project.

Tom Marazzo

Tom Marazzo

....

Allan Cunningham
Amanda Lakhanpal
Andrea Schroder
Anna G.
Bogdan Coman
Brenda Williams
Brian B.
Bruce Forsyth
Carla Brown
Cathy Smith
Charlene Myers
Chris Shaw
Christian Laurin
Claire Dossantos
Crystalyn Zucchetto
Damien Michaud
Darcy S. Van Horn
David and Erika Sloan
David McKay
Dena Jacoubsen
Duncan James Webster
Edith Rizzi
Elaine B.
Ella Secara
Emily Schroeder
Fern Comeau
Gary Oosterhof
Iain Fraser
Ian Wilkie
Ivana
Jason Bouwman
Jason Lavigne
Jason Marceau
Jeffrey Armitage
Jim Stachow
Joan Higgs
Jo-Ann Collins
Joann Willis

JoAnne Smith, UK
John Karasinski
Julie Gayer
Karen Kimmett
Kimberly Neuman
Lisa Wilz
Lynn Bishop
Margaret Rempel
Margareta Mina
Mary Henderson
Michael Lapierre
Michael and Tammy Polson
Miriam Bartley
Naura Wolfe
Nicole Evans
Nicole Hawley
Olson Ryan
Pascal Belisle
Rachel Aubin
Ray McGinnis
Rick Sproull
Rita Smith
Sam Ross
Steve Venright
Susan Westersund
Tanya McKee
Thomas Kuntz
Tom Fabian

Manufactured by Amazon.ca
Bolton, ON

35872644R00157